THE JACK PREGER STORY

FOR JACK,

KALA

and

THE FLYOVER PEOPLE

The Jack Preger Story

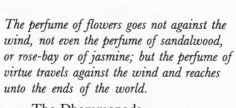

The perfume of flowers goes not against the wind, not even the perfume of sandalwood, or rose-bay or of jasmine; but the perfume of virtue travels against the wind and reaches unto the ends of the world.

The Dhammapada

Frances Meigh

TABB HOUSE

First published 1988
Tabb House, 7 Church Street, Padstow, Cornwall, PL28 8BG

—

The copyrights of the illustrations belong to the author except for those with the owners
named on the List of Illustrations.

Typeset by St. George Typesetting, Redruth, Cornwall
Printed in Great Britain by T. J. Press (Padstow) Ltd.

Contents

Acknowledgements

I would like to thank all those who have made this book possible, both in India and England, together with Dr Jack Preger who has been patient when others would have been exasperated over supplying detailed information, Countess Badeni and Mrs Ruth Lumley-Smith for their help in reading the manuscript, friends who have had to put up with me while it was being written, my friend and secretary Daphne Bruton for endless typing and advice, and the librarians I have consulted. I am also grateful to journalists and photographers for their constant support for Dr Preger's work, and to organisations, societies and private individuals for their interest in the story — to them all, my thanks.

Frances Meigh

List of Plates

The photograph of Dr Preger on the front of the book's dust jacket and illustrations nos. 8 and 17 are by Allen Jewhurst of Chameleon Films, taken for the Channel Four TV film *34 Middleton Row; The Jack Preger Story,* and are reproduced by courtesy of Chameleon Films. No. 6 is reproduced by courtesy of *The Telegraph*, Calcutta. The drawings are by Frances Meigh.

PROLOGUE

My head was opened by the sudden touch of the Spirit and the words 'Become a Doctor' were put in. Then it closed again

Dr Jack Preger

PROLOGUE

OUTSIDE, the London air was clear and clean, the pavements almost dry, after early morning rain. The pale stone of the Church of St Columba was as brilliant as a Giotto fresco and the traffic almost non-existent, when I opened the heavy front door of the Challoner Club, early on a June morning in 1982. I had come to meet Jack Preger, with whom I worked in India. He stood on the step, a suitcase beside him and a grip bag in his hand, both heavy and packed for the return trip to India that he would make in a few hours' time. After a special journey to England from the sub-continent to see his sick mother and family he was going back to the heat, the simple life, and the poor. His poor, his patients, who under the relentless sun of that far land were waiting for him, and for the help that he gave them. By living out his destiny in Calcutta, and working endlessly with the destitutes who crowd the pavements, disused railway lines, shacks, gutters, the spaces under bridges and flyovers in that 'City of Dreadful Night',[1] he has given them a chance of their condition being changed; for he is their doctor, Dr Jack Preger.

THE turning point in Jack Preger's life and the beginning of the road to his service for the poor were the charismatic experiences that pushed him out of farming and into medicine, and later out of hospital in Armagh, Northern Ireland, to Dacca or Dhaka, as it is now spelt, and ultimately to Calcutta.

It was in Wales, in 1964, when he was farming Gernos Farm at St Dogmaels, Pembrokeshire, that after much prayer and thought, Jack Preger asked God to give him one positive sign of His existence and promised, if He did, that the rest of his life

---

1. *City of Dreadful Night* was the name given by Rudyard Kipling to a volume of short stories about Calcutta.

would be God's, to do with as He wished.

He got the sign. At that time Jack Preger was not a Christian, but one evening in the farmhouse kitchen he was drawn to read some verses from the New Testament: St Paul's letter to the Romans, chapter II, verses 25-26. It was as a fellow Jew to Jacob Preger that St Paul reached him with the words 'A deliverer shall come from Sion, to rid Jacob of his unfaithfulness'. The words had the effect of showing him, with absolute clarity, that he had to leave his Jewish religion and, as he interpreted it, be rid thereby of what he now saw as his unfaithfulness. And so it was that after reading the extract he very soon became Jack Preger, a Christian and a Roman Catholic.

That was the first of four events that were instrumental in bringing about a total commitment to what is now his work in India.

Abbot William Thierry, in *The Golden Epistle*, analysing St Paul, writing to the Philippians, chapter III, verses 12–15, talks of the 'stretching forward to those things that are the perfection of the just man in this life' and of the apprehension and understanding and holding on to truth as he sees it; and subsequently the continual acting on it. These actions hold the key to perseverance. There is the same stress in the *Dhammapada*[2] and in the *I Ching*[3]. All repeat what every balanced person from the schoolroom to the grave would surely accept as constituents of a fundamental discipline for the achievement of success in any field and, in the case in question, for the emergence of a new life with its difficulties and seeming contradictions: the common denominators of perseverance, persistence and resoluteness.

There was another dramatic moment in Jack Preger's life, in 1964, one which he recalls as most important and moving; an encounter set against a backcloth of Pembrokeshire landscape. On a steep track where there were sheep on the hillside round him, whose bleating cries permeated everything, all day and all night, he was driving a tractor, doing ordinary everyday work, when an order was put into his mind, as though, he says, "my head was opened by the sudden touch of the Spirit" although at the time he had no idea what it was, "and the words,

2. The *Dhammapada*. A collection of aphorisms illustrating the Buddhist moral law.
3. The *I Ching*, or *Book of Changes*. Chinese Book of Oracles.

'BECOME A DOCTOR' were put in. Then it closed again.''

That evening after work he wrote to medical colleges and teaching hospitals, seeking admission to study medicine. He was thirty-four years old.

These first mystical experiences; the offer of his life, the subsequent reading and later the order; were powerful and lasting. He has followed them ever since — recognising, listening, and acting in obedience to his understanding of them.

WHEN circumstances change, and actualities that correspond to someone's deepest desires coincide, then there is all at once an excess of strength available to that person. It causes a coming together of the person as a whole. This in turn brings with it all that is needed to continue in the path. It is the force of the Holy Spirit perhaps, and it is a path, although one that is not at first necessarily clearly apparent to the individual, but can be seen as such later when looking back, by which time a pattern has emerged.

These charismatic experiences, as Jack calls them, are a living part of his present life and they were the starting point, keystone, and foundation of his work in India. His total commitment to this work has great simplicity and strength of purpose because it is grounded in an unswerving and constant reference to the power of God and the Holy Spirit. It is inspired still further by the splendour of St Paul, and it is irreversible. He accepts with Pauline courage that if prison is the inevitable consequence of his actions in West Bengal, where the present government objects to his work for the sick and dying, then he will go to prison for however long it must be. Yet imprisonment would bring his work to a halt and his people would suffer because of it.

THAT evening in 1964, motivated by profound experience, he wrote letters that bore fruit, and Jack Preger was accepted as a student at the Royal College of Surgeons in Dublin. He graduated from there in 1971, after which he went on to St Lawrence's Hospital, also in Dublin, to complete his internship. It was after that, in 1972, that he heard a wireless appeal for doctors and nurses to go out to Bangladesh to work for refugees in the camps there, and it was an appeal to which he responded.

3

Dr Preger went first to Dacca where he worked at the Children's Hospital, and the Bihari Refugee Camps of Mohammedpur. From 1973-1974 he worked with 'Concern' and from 1975-1979 with 'Terre des Hommes' at the Dispensary in Dacca, and at the International Boys' Town. From 1976-1979 he was Director of the Khan Sahib Azizul Islam Memorial Hospital for Destitutes in Dacca.

AFTER the experience in Wales, at Castle Leslie, County Monaghan, in Ireland, there was another encounter at Pentecost. This time the Paraclete announced Himself: 'I am the Paraclete'. At that time Jack Preger remembers he did not know what the Paraclete meant, and had to look it up in a dictionary. The Oxford English Dictionary definition is Advocate, and quotes St John Chapter XIV, v. 16 and 26: 'If you love me you will obey my commands; and I will ask the Father, and he will give you another to be your Advocate. . . the Holy Spirit whom the Father will send in my name will teach you everything, and will call to mind all I have told you!

In Calcutta, in February 1982, Dr Preger told me of an event that was really the culmination of the first three. He was reminded of it as we passed a female fortune teller, her parrot beside her, as she sat cross-legged on the pavement in the dusty and crowded street, next to an exuberant handkerchief hawker. We were with the *Daily Telegraph* journalist, Charles Nevin, who had come to cover the court hearing to which we were going. The court buildings were at the end of the same road, so possibly it was a good pitch for those who wished to know their futures. Jack remarked that the sight of her reminded him of some unforgettable words that he was given in 1973, from a similar fortune teller in Bangladesh. These fortune tellers can often be seen on the streets in India, sitting on rattan mats, small brilliant green parrots beside them held in restricting wooden cages. A straight line of little envelopes is laid out on the pavement in front of the door to the cages. When there is a client the door is unlatched carefully and the bird is freed, its claws awkward on the flat ground. It chooses an envelope, picking it up in one sideways movement of the beak. This is then taken from the bird by the fortune teller, who from her place on the mat hands it up to the client. When Jack Preger opened the selected envelope he found a note inside written in

4

Hindi, which, translated, said 'You should work for the poor'. This happened when he had no particular job in Bangladesh. It was, he recalls, 'an added push'.

Clearly, his continuing source of strength is related to this sequence of experiences and encounters.

DRIVING along on our way to the airport on that June morning in 1982, we talked of the future, for there could be no going back, only a forging ahead with all the work that was and is to be achieved in Calcutta. We went through the tunnel to the departure section of the airport. The lights glowed orange, the way was quite clear, there were no bodies lying by the roadside, no women washing dishes or bowls in the puddles, no one dying — only clear pavements under the bridge.

"You must remember this," I said, "when you are under the flyover."

"Do you mean because there are no destitutes?" the doctor asked.

"Yes, because there are no destitutes." I was imagining that this was the place (only tiny in comparison) under Howrah Bridge in Calcutta where many of the ever-increasing numbers of Dr Preger's patients live; but there, in that country of brilliant sunlight, under that other bridge, all appears black. The filth is deep, and pigs thread their way among the patients; the children's tears streak pale paths down dark Bengali skin; hope and expectation of life stretches no further than the next handful of rice and a swim in the murky and polluted Ganges.

All these thoughts were still going through my mind when later, the luggage checked in, we sat talking. Then it was time for Jack to go, we did not know for how long; for by returning to the Communist State of West Bengal in India Dr Preger was facing a possible prison sentence of five years. Simply, and with a gentle smile, he paused briefly before filing past the officials to the formalities of immigration and customs, to the paraphernalia of travel, and to at least eighteen hours flying time, for his return to the exhausting rounds of the Calcutta sick, and to all that fate might have in store.

As I waved to his plane from the airport roof, I remembered my own journeys to India, to Calcutta, and the events that had led to my working with Dr Preger. It seemed that many things were involved, things over which no-one ever has control: a sea of events or of troubles perhaps, destiny, life, through which we pass, touching here or there something that turns us in our tracks and leaves us different people, changed. Are these things to be hoarded in our minds like dusty lace in an attic or shared with others, who may find in them something of value? Here, then, is my story, in which you may find, as I have, reflected in the work of the doctor, the spirit of truth and the strength of freedom.

CHAPTER I

CALCUTTA

> *In the face of each and every man, above all when tears and suffering has rendered it transparent, we witness the face of Christ Himself*

Prior of Taizé quoting Pope Paul VI

CHAPTER I

England, March 1981

H OAR blossom turned English beeches into the drooping ornamental trees of a Chinese print; the sky was not separate from the fields and there was no horizon. The landscape lay as still as my frozen breath on the windscreen of the little green car while I drove through the blank whiteness and the bitter cold of the early March morning. I was travelling alone, at the start of a series of journies that were to take me thousands of miles. Later I was to travel in trains overflowing with people, both inside and outside; on the footplates — clinging, sitting, and lying — while the untouchables, with their pathetic cloth bundles, scampered precariously along the carriage roofs; rattling across India, through the intense heat of the plains of the vast sub-continent, in trains that never seemed to stop. I was to travel in aeroplanes over the North West Frontier from Kabul in Afghanistan to Delhi, on buses over mountain passes to Nepal, in laden rickshaws over the frontiers of India, and even packed into an oxen cart balancing my typewriter (aptly named a traveller-de-luxe model) on the top of the rest of my baggage. That was along the wide, flat road in Tamil Nadu, from the railway station at Kalithalai on the way to the ashram of Dom Bede Griffiths at Thannir Palli three miles on, with only a metal hook fastened across the back of the cart to stop me from falling onto the road.

These journeys were to take me from North to South and three times across and back in a country that I was to come to love, as I love England; India.

THE flight was Air India, economy class. We landed four

9

times *en route* and were due to arrive in Calcutta at 10.30 on a Monday night, March 16th, 1981. Crossing Europe, it had become progressively colder as we flew through the night, but the sun as we reached the Arabian Gulf was brilliant and hot. In my hand-luggage were the drugs that Sister Celine of the Missionaries of Charity's London House had brought to Heathrow airport at the last minute, when with another sister she had come to see me off. Like nearly all the Order's nuns they were Indians and wore navy blue cardigans over their cotton saris, with distinctive blue lines at the edge.

The drugs were for Mother Teresa. There had been smiles from the check-out staff as we pushed the bottles and jars into the spaces I had left for them in my luggage. Now all that was already many hours behind me.

AS I left the plane the heat of the Indian night met me, and the stillness. After the usual formalities I went with my trolley into the main entrance where porters and taxi drivers abound. I got both, but before leaving I had to change some travellers cheques, as rupees are unobtainable outside India. Without change it was not even possible to tip one rupee per piece to the porter who waited beside me hoping for more. The banking transaction completed, I got into my first Calcutta taxi. It was dark outside, but I could make out palm trees and buildings, and, not far off, the lights of the tall Airport Hotel where I was to stay.

In the large bedroom it was quiet and stuffy, the air through the internal air-conditioning stale and the windows, heavy with double glazing, not meant to open. I stared out through the dull glass. The lights of the hotel car park lit the palm trees from above; they looked like an orange-filtered photograph in an out-of-season dusty tourist office. There was little to see, for Dum Dum Airport is well out of Calcutta, at the end of the VIP Road, notorious for armed robbery.

The whole place felt muffled, as if the sound had been turned down but the house telephone worked so I ordered tea, and a plug for the bath — the deep sided bath which, after twenty-six hours in airports and on aeroplanes, it was my most fervent desire to get into. A heavily-turbanned bearer brought the tea, and a twist of cloth, which he pushed into the empty plug hole. It held, and the bath filled. This was, after all, a four star hotel!

I took some thin clothes carefully from the top of my case for the morning. I had arranged for a taxi at 8 a.m. so that I could take the urgently-needed drugs straight to the Mother House.

Tired, but awake, I wrote off six letters to relatives and friends, to mail from the hotel in the morning, for it would save me time not having to find a post office. At last, as a result of the stale air, lack of oxygen, or whatever it was that was being circulated through the system of the expensive but safe hotel, I slept through what was left of my first night in India.

ERRATIC and fast, my taxi tore along the straight road into Calcutta, then penetrated further into the city, which was choked with dilapidated buses, rickshaws, people, full pavements, and streetsellers. There were people whichever way you looked and the air was heavy with fumes. The driver knew the way, thank heaven. Later I was to find many who did not. It was a help that in London I had been warned of how much I would have to pay. This was a city where I needed to know as much as possible, and quickly.

At the side of a building along the Lower Circular Road was a narrow passage; a few steps along it there were double wooden doors, with a cross on one of them; beside it in the doorway the number 54A, and below it a wooden frame with a name 'Mother Teresa IN/OUT'. It read OUT.

Inside, a black house-dog pulled on its chain, barking and straining; the courtyard was cool, its surrounding walls high, the city beyond its gates. Stone seats lined the walls. Plants grew in one corner, another held a Lourdes-like grotto built around a blue-sashed and white-robed statue of the Virgin. On the first floor there was a balcony with the chapel, and other rooms opening off it. The stairs leading to the chapel were opposite the grotto.

A woman in a coloured sari answered the door bell and led me past the boisterous dog to a small room with two doorways giving onto the courtyard, and left me to wait.

I looked at the pale blue aerogramme with the Indian stamp, crumpled and thin, that was my 'Letter of Credit'. A few weeks earlier I had written to Mother Teresa, and it was her authorised reply that I held in my hand. In my letter I had told her things that I had experienced and thought, things I had not discussed with anyone else, and had asked her advice about whether I should work for her in India. Her answer had tipped

11

the balance. 'However difficult and impractical it may seem, go on. You cannot deny Him in humility and faith'.

With this letter another world was unfolded to me, a world within a world. Originally my eyes had been opened by the death of a friend who, in the act of dying, had inexplicably exposed an awareness of another set of definitions of life, other values, which threw everything that I believed to be reality on its head, and changed the face of the world. It was to make life in the accepted sense of the word unreal, and it was this burning unreality of existence that led me to ask myself, over and over again: 'What am I doing here?'

Many people have sought the answer to this question. It was in order to try to find the key that I had been impelled to travel the thousands of miles to Calcutta, to the Mother House of the Missionaries of Charity. Here, off a busy street in a city that I did not know, I had arrived to do what I must — because I could no longer do anything else.

In the face of suffering it is possible to encounter Christ, the 'Man in men'. The Prior of Taizé said this in his book *Violent for Peace* which I later found, in 1983, in the guesthouse library of the Carmelite Monastery at Presteigne. I could see then that what I had tried to write to Mother Teresa is expressed with clarity in this book. For Roger Schutz, the Prior of Taizé, quoting Pope Paul VI, writes about the encounter between man and Christ: 'When this encounter occurs we are filled with awe. But we cannot rest there. Before long we are called by another demand to encounter man, even the man who does not share our faith. Because in the face of each and every man "above all when tears and suffering have rendered it transparent", we witness the face of Christ Himself.'

It was this experience, this same encounter, that I had dimly experienced. I had glimpsed it in hospital in the face of the man I loved, who, before his tragic accident, had wanted us both to do something for people — for the poor. He was not certain how or in what manner, but he often talked about Dr Coggan's concept of 'putting your arms round the world'. Since then, over the years, many people of perception and insight have understood, as I came to understand before he died, that one purpose of his mutely-endured suffering was that I should also understand what he already knew.

Any work I have done in India had its beginnings in that

12

suffering. For the use of suffering is to try to change the face of the world.

THE walls of the room where I waited were covered with framed documents, giving details of the Order and its constitution. There were diagrams of the world, scored with telltale spots, indicating the presence of its other houses, now operating in fifty-three different countries. There was a touching photograph of Mother Teresa with the present Pope (Pope John Paul II).

Suddenly some sisters appeared. Yes, they told me, they were expecting the medicines. Was I tired? I must have some breakfast. They gave me toast, tea, bananas, and butter with a particular flavour that ever since I have associated with the Mother House. It was like being in a room full of white birds, all chattering away in English, the language of the house. One of the sisters took charge of the drugs, another brought the tray; Sister Henrietta sat at the head of the table, her hands clasped in front of her, while Mother Teresa's second-in-command read the letter which I'd brought her. I gave them the bulky parcel of disposable syringes that I'd bought at a branch of Boots, on Paddington Station. There were also letters and books from Sister Marie Celine, newspapers as well, including the biggest glossy magazine that I could find on Prince Charles, in whom Mother Teresa was very interested. Later I heard that all the nuns were delighted with this.

They whirled away with the assorted items, and I was given an escort of two sisters, who took me by taxi to the YWCA's International Guest House in Middleton Row, open now to both sexes, reliable, clean, and, of course, safe from armed robbery.

I was told to rest for twenty-four hours, and then to come back at 8 a.m., when I could go in the ambulance with Sister Luke (in charge at the Home for the Dying, *Nirmal Hriday*, at Kalighat) where I was to work. This is what I had asked to be allowed to do.

There is no provision for staying with the sisters although the brothers (Missionaries of Charity) do have male guests to stay with them.

The room I was allotted at the YMCA was quite an experience. It cost about thirty-six pounds a month with full board. A cubicle-type room, the walls open from about eight feet up, it had a very simple bed, dressing table, and a built-in cupboard. There was a padlock on the outside of the door, and a bolt on the inside. There was no mosquito net. I bought this later at the Newmarket market.

The sisters had worked hard to obtain my room, patiently insistent, wearing down the reluctance of the formidable secretary, who did not wish to accept me. Later I realised this was the normal procedure.

The mosquito net I bought was too expensive — but it was a good one. I fixed it up to the wooden T-shaped extension above the bed with a bit of string. There was a rather grimy fan, but immobile; power cuts last for several hours on end, load shedding; so I wrote more letters, and had a shower.

My few valuables, my return ticket and passport, address book and photographs, I put in my suitcase. I locked it, covering it with carelessly-strewn newspapers and an old bedcover that was in the cupboard for I had been told that people scaled the bedroom walls. I changed the door lock, buying an excellent gleaming brass padlock with an individual lock from the nearby Jubilee Stores in Park Street. I put the key on a cord around my neck, and never lost anything, unlike many people. I have bought padlocks in all sizes, for doors, suitcases, and cupboards.

After deciding that it would be better to sleep well that night rather than attempt to sleep in the day (besides, it was exciting to be actually in Calcutta), I looked around the 'Y'. There seemed to be a lot of visitors of all nationalities, including Iranians, French, Maltese and Indian. There were tennis courts (used mostly by outsiders) where it would have been good to have had a garden. The dining-room had several long tables (it was a hostel really) where Indian lunches were served, and European dinners; tea was from 4 till 5.30 p.m.

There was a pleasant sweeper on the first floor, who cleaned my room out. From reception I acquired sheets, a pillow case, and a very thin abrasive towel. The mattress of my bed was stuffed with coconut fibres, and from one corner dust poured out. When I expressed concern over this, Bharat, who was to become a devoted friend over the years, marched solemnly out with it over his shoulder, and came back with another. There was a second bed in my tiny room, but I had a horror of sharing, so Bharat took that away, also.

Outside in the passage there was a large table with a lot of junk on it, pushed against a wall. I touched it, thinking it would make an admirable desk. Bharat, whose intuition rarely failed, shunted it through the narrow door into my room. Progress, I felt, had been made.

That afternoon I went to Shishu Bhavan, Mother Teresa's Children's Home in Lower Circular Road, not far from the Mother House. I walked there in order to know the way the next morning. Shishu was full of children and babies of all ages. The premature ones are sad, with tiny little bodies and deep-set dark eyes which, disconcertingly adult, look at you in the most intelligent way. What will their futures be?

One child had had a cerebral ulcer when, if his head was tipped one way, pus would run from the ear. Now this child has been cured though the sister in attendance said she didn't know how, as the doctors had given up hope.

Many of the children were going to be adopted. Indian women worked at Shishu Bhavan alongside the sisters, and were fed there in return for their work.

AT seven in the morning on the following day I went to the Mother House. A sentimental blue and gold religious card showing the Madonna and Child was stuck on the sun shade on the driver's side of Mother Teresa's ambulance, which, serving as a bus, presently jerked and jarred its way along the Calcutta streets to Kalighat at 7.45 a.m. The heat was already oppressive, and the smell of the city was relentlessly present. We sat, six at each side, in the simple blue-painted interior of the ambulance. The white saris of the novices contrasted sharply with their black eyes. Hands clutched at the seats as the driver lurched at the traffic lights, and fingers felt for their rosary beads as they prayed, in charming English, the Hail Mary. Another day had begun.

Sister Luke sat opposite me. She said little, but her personality was impressive. When she did speak it was to call out an order to the driver.

Kalighat was formerly the resting place for pilgrims visiting the Kalighat Temple next to it. The Temple is dedicated to the goddess Kali, from which the name Calcutta is derived. Inside its walls the temple pavements run with the blood of sacrificed goats, killed by the permanently fixed, curved blade in one of its courtyards, while women file past, unconcerned, to touch the fertility tree, which is worn smooth and leafless by the barren

15

fingers of generations. Outside, priests of the temple offer guided tours.

Kalighat was given to Mother Teresa by the authorities some years ago, when she asked them for somewhere to accommodate the dying. We went up the few steps, brushing between the street traders' stalls that fringe the entrance. Many photographs have been taken in the interior of Kalighat, perhaps the most famous of these being the one that illustrated Malcolm Muggeridge's book on Mother Teresa and her work. This photograph was singled out because of its remarkable clarity. It came out perfectly, in spite of the camera-man's insistence that there was not enough light to attempt a shot at all.

Nothing really prepares you for Kalighat, although it is exactly as one has seen it portrayed. The patients on their low beds dominate the scene, while everyone is aware of the spirit of dedication of those who tend them, although the nuns do not remain there for the whole twenty-four hours of every day. This is because their work as members of a contemplative order necessitates their return to the Mother House for their other work of prayer.

Inside, the building is roughly divided into two halves. The male ward is on your left as you enter, and on the right there is a raised area with cupboards for drugs, books, records, and a very simple desk. This open part acts as an open office.

The cooking takes place on the lower level, where there is a furnace. It is used to cook the enormous quantities of rice, dahl, chapattis, and omelettes that are needed to provide meals for the patients. I have cooked over the tremendous heat of those red coals until I thought it would be impossible ever to be cool again. To the right is the women's ward. In the centre, accessible through open archways, is the bathing area, the water and the taps. There are raised slabs used for bathing the patients on. The taps are plugged with bandages as they do not actually turn off; the flow is simply staunched.

The beds are low, the patients being little more than a foot from the floor; bedhooks are used to move them about. They have heavy oilskin covers over the mattresses, and are covered with a blue sheet knotted underneath with a double knot. All the plastic undersheets are scrubbed each day and the sheets changed. The terrazzo flooring is scrubbed with ashes and cinders; cleaning it is a tremendous operation that rips one's fingers to shreds.

16

The walls and the ceiling are painted blue, and near the entrance doors there is a little altar and a large picture of Mother Teresa, which tends to get moved about. Nearby there is a crucifix that I particularly liked, with an unusual figure, and next to it the painted words: 'I THIRST'.

On the women's side there is a row of remarkable windows that take about two hours to clean. You set to work with two bowls of water, piling up all the glass on an unused bed. One day, having finished the windows, I asked the sister if there was anything else that she would like done. She answered "No — just love them!"

The sick and the dying watch you. That was the first thing that I was aware of. Their eyes are often sunk, dark and clouded. Those who are very sick — almost gone — are placed close to the centre, the raised area, so that they can be watched all the time. Those on drips are also near the entrance, close to Sister Luke. The small mortuary is off the bathing section in the middle, but I only saw that much later on, after the death of Rabeya. Her story is a sad one, but then all the stories are sad. The very fact that the people are here is itself the worst, and paradoxically the best, that can happen to them. They have been brought in off the pavements of this beautiful and terrible city, with its incredible contrasts of misery and courage. For me this is the one city in the world where I feel completely alive. The life-and-death element is so overpowering that there is no halfway.

THE old woman I was feeding had died. She died of malnutrition. I was told to feed her after we had finished doing the beds. I thought that she was not well enough to eat, and at one point I fetched Sister Luke. There was nothing she could do. Really I was just sitting with her for company; she looked old, but as she was suffering from malnutrition she was probably younger than she actually looked. She gazed steadily at me. I put my arm under her light body at her shoulders. . . then she died. We wrapped her in a shroud and she was taken to the mortuary. Three others died the same night.

That happened on my first morning at Kalighat.

On another day Santi died. She looked simply beautiful, exquisite, lying in a white sari, with a rose border, her eyes slightly open — quite peaceful — and holding in her most lovely hands the now withered and fading roses that Pauline

Smithson, a British television production manager, who worked in Kalighat and of whom Santi was very fond, had given her when she left. Her gold-coloured bangles were bright on her dusky skin. She epitomised India, its death in life, its beauty and despair, its past and present and future. Around her gathered children, crying, and Jasolda, mother of one of the families that lived on the roof at Kalighat, who had suffered facial burns, stood on the raised area looking down, her pale and damaged eyes wet. Sister Luke sat naturally at Santi's feet talking to them all.

Then Bubula, a boy from the roof area came down to get me for his English lesson. Life goes relentlessly on.

CHAPTER II

KALIGHAT

Never let anything so fill your heart with sorrow as to make you forget the joy of Christ risen

Painted on the staircase wall of the Mother House of the Missionaries of Charity

CHAPTER II

Kalighat 1981

TRAMLINES caught the rickshaw wheels, the lights reflected off the wet and shining cobbles as the trams closed in behind us, and a girl walked idly across our path, to be shouted at as we narrowly missed her. The impetus of the rickshaw sending us quickly by, her reply was drowned in the hooting of horns and the now-heavier fall of rain. It was late and I was in a hurry to get to the Assembly of God Hospital.

The rain increased and lightning zigzagged. The rickshaw man turned up a side street, where children busily raked out the cinders of the bucket braziers, and dogs lay flat, like rugs, exhausted by the heat of the day. The rickshaw turned in at the hospital entrance as the rain turned to a torrential sheet, making the rupees for the rickshaw man wet in my hand. Then the heavy glass door shut quietly behind me. The errand uppermost in my mind obscured the scene and focused only on the softly-lighted enquiry counter. I asked for Dr Sylvester.

"He is there." The receptionist indicated a figure standing, arms folded, by the Emergency sign of the Casualty Department. He was watching me, and I went over to give him the message I had brought from the Mother House, to ask if the hospital could keep the body of a lovely young girl who had died, tragically, that afternoon. Rabeya was a house girl, a servant, only twenty-six and the mother of three children.

As we talked I began to realise that I was being forced into a position where I was either going to have to take the initiative or remain extremely firm. Disposing of the body of a young Moslem woman who had died in a highly toxic condition, and

21

doing so, moreover, at 8.30 on a storm-racked night in Calcutta, was likely to be a difficult, even dangerous, undertaking. To this I could now add, according to the doctor, the complication that she had also had typhoid. The hospital authorities plainly did not wish to keep the body as the risk of infection was too great, and they had already done their part free of charge for Mother Teresa. They had admitted her a week earlier, and operated on her for peritonitis, and an exploratory investigation.

She had been in poor condition then, also suffering from suspected TB, which was later confirmed. Her chances were small. I had been with her every morning and afternoon for a week. In the evenings her relatives visited her there, in one of Calcutta's best hospitals. My thoughts went back to when she was first at Kalighat, her beautiful face imploring and worried, always wanting Sister Luke to see her. When she was admitted to the Assembly of God hospital, because she was so nervous and highly strung Sister Luke asked me to stay with her in the daytime. The chance that she would not make it was always there.

Her room in Ward E was narrow. There was a window with a grill at the far end, and two beds along the righthand side wall. Rabeya's was nearest the window, and at the foot of hers was the other, in which an old, rather distinguished-looking woman lay, suffering from a broken hip. On the bedside table were large exotic pink flowers pushed into an old medicine bottle. Rabeya's sheets were stained from her wound which was seeping and her intravenous drip often ran low. I watched it, fetching the nurse whenever it got to the last inch or two, when a new bottle was hung up. The staff came to know me while I was attending Rabeya, the receptionist who nodded me past the armed guard at the bottom of the stairs, and finally the doctors and nurses on the ward. I had briefly met her sister one evening when a large priest came round saying prayers in a heavy, trembling voice and then without a word drifted away.

The day she died I left her for an hour in the morning; on my return she was intensely excited, wanting to return to Kalighat. Everytime she saw me that was what she asked for, not the attention of a remarkably good hospital staff, but Kalighat. Something in her reached out for peace, knowing that beyond the frontiers of medicine and drips and science was that priceless item, love, which is all, perhaps, that the human race

22

wants, and does not realise. What Rabeya, the beautiful Moslem girl, did know and want was the love that the Home for the Dying could give. She tore the oxygen tube away from her face and held tightly to my hands.

"Take me with you — only take me back, oh Mother, oh Allah. . ." Sadly, it was not possible.

Now she was gone — to find the peace and joy that she longed for, leaving me to dispose of her empty body.

So there we stood, and I realised that we had now reached the mechanics of the situation, the life having left it. This emphasised to me how completely real the spirit, or soul, of a person is for, as the rain squalled and the lightning continued its erratic progress across the night sky, Rabeya appeared to have gone before the storm, and the body we were discussing had become an empty object that was to be respected but was nevertheless quite, quite empty.

I declined firmly Dr Sylvester's proposal that I should hand over the case to a funeral parlour. I said I was a Christian, Rabeya a Moslem. Her relatives would not be pleased and it would cause difficulties. He understood. But, he reiterated, he could not keep the body. Then, I said, he must tell the Missionaries of Charity. "May I use your telephone to call them?" I asked. I particularly wanted him to give his decision to them direct, although earlier I had been instructed to deal with the hospital myself, which was why I had had to brave the storm in order to see the doctor. Now I managed to get through to Sister Luke, and put the doctor on to her. It was finally arranged that the Missionaries of Charity's ambulance would collect the body and take it in the early morning to Kalighat. So she would return after all, and be kept there for her relatives to claim. When they called at the hospital, they would be sent on to the Missionaries of Charity who, in turn, would refer them to Sister Luke at Kalighat.

The next day the relatives did not appear for some time at the hospital. Sister Luke was most concerned. Whatever happened, if they had not come by that evening the Moslem undertakers would have to bury her. The ambulance was scheduled to take the body to them at lunchtime. Fortunately however, it broke down, and it was then that the relatives did arrive. Until then the body had been in the little mortuary, where I saw her just once more, at her beloved Kalighat.

One morning when I had to see Mother Teresa about a

23

young girl who lived with her family on the roof at Kalighat I understood why Sister Luke found her so calming and simply decisive. We were discussing the case of Chanandra, a fourteen-year-old girl with a heart defect. Tests had shown that she had a hole in her heart. I had had to visit the Cardiology Department at the P. G. Hospital. Then I found the consulting room in its usual dusty state. An Indian nursing sister sat at a table in her stiffly-pleated sari with crimson epaulets, reading the newspaper. In front of her were countless pieces of paper with the rubber stamped name of the hospital in one corner. She was ready for the day.

I sat next to the Registrar of the Chief Surgeon. He was small and quick, and on the few occasions that I had been to this department with patients we had usually talked for a while. Today was no exception. I negotiated with the Registrar for a free bed for Chanandra, and also for free surgery. We made good progress; he accepted her and agreed to admit her for the operation. The only things that he could not provide would be supplied by Mother Teresa's Missionaries of Charity. They would include blood, an oxygenator, and post-operative medicine. If Chanandra did not have the operation she would probably die within ten years, and as deterioration would set in shortly, weakening the lungs and lessening the chances of success, it was vital that she be admitted as soon as possible.

Later after Mass one morning at the Mother House I put the alternatives to Mother. She was direct: "You have done the work, she has a place. Now it is up to God whether she lives or dies, that is all. It is nothing to worry about."

Chanandra has long since had the operation, and is now recovered and fit.

There were other times when Mother Teresa said things that were to stick in my mind. One of them was the day after Santi died. We were going up the stairs to the Chapel at the Mother House. It was the eve of a general strike. I was with another volunteer, an American girl, a friend, who was at that time an auctioneer with Sothebys in New York. She was good looking and always well dressed. Mother Teresa came alongside us on the stairs and took Lorna's hand, and held it up.

"Take it off," she said, pointing to the nail varnish, and I thought 'Oh, don't look at my toenails.' She repeated "Take it off and use the money for the poor; its expensive."

"But it keeps up my morale," Lorna replied.

24

"Keep it on then, keep it on!" said Mother.

One day, after chapel, Sister Luke told us not to go to Kalighat the next day. Because of the general strike there could be trouble. (As it turned out several buses were burnt). We agreed not to, and started back to the Y. We got as far as Lower Circular Road when suddenly everyone was running. The little shops slammed down their shutters and someone shouted that the police were firing into the crowd. We ran faster. I called to Lorna to turn off down the first right hand turn, and we ran down the side street to safety. Afterwards we were told that someone had let off a bomb.

Each working day started early with the walk to Chowringhee Road at the top of Park Street, to wait for the single decker No. 76 bus to Kalighat. I waited amongst the piles of dried and dusty earth and stones, the fruit of the never-ending excavations for the 'metro', and the holes that filled with water during the monsoon and became deathtraps. On the way up Park Street I used to pass the street traders setting up their stalls for the day's trading. With infinite care on rickety card tables they stacked up cigarette packets, fountain pens, biros, lighters, all carried to their pitch in suitcases. Most of them had a small boy who always knew where everything was, and who had already inherited his life's work. Always they tried to sell you American cigarettes, as these were the most expensive, and foreign soap. Even so early in the day, the wind blew hotly in my face. I felt clammy and warm, and glad when the bus came, so long as it was not too crowded. There were jasmine flowers made into a garland in front of the goddess painted over the seat reserved for ladies, just behind the driver. They swung about as the bus accelerated and jerked its way down the road to Kalighat, until it reached the fire station. Just after that was the stop where I used to get off, and walk round the corner, passing the scraggy sacred black cow having its breakfast out of a bucket at one of the street stalls. The dogs all looked the same. One had mange, and had no coat at all. The rats were big, and dead ones lay in the streets; dead dogs too, and goats slept on the pavements as well. One little shop was always stuffed with straw, I suppose for the cow. Soon I came to know the smiling street sellers.

Often I asked myself if I was mad to be working in Calcutta. The heat, the dirt, the squalor, misery and disease, were always there, not in the wings but in the open streets, where children

25

with malaria slept drenched in sweat, a begging bowl beside them.

The leaking sewer in Park Street flowed continually across the pavement during all the years I spent in Calcutta, and women passers-by delicately picked their way over it, their exquisite saris lifted above the flow. Next to it lay a sleeping beggar woman and her child, who would perhaps in his adult life remember the street where he had lived. With, dare one say, affection? It is, after all, one of the best streets in Calcutta.

There were other things, such as the frustration of queues at post offices, where Indian female clerks slowly thumbed their way through dusty ledgers, looking up the price of a stamp for the next Province. If one tried to hurry them they seemed to delight in lingering even longer over their grimy ledgers.

DR Jack Preger had been on leave in England when I first arrived in Calcutta, so I heard about his work long before meeting him. After his return he came to Kalighat to ask for news of Santi, who had died during his absence, and I met him then for the first time.

One Saturday morning Dr Jack Preger asked me if I could take a patient to the Plastic Surgery Clinic which was being held that day. The patient was a man called Kala Pradhan. Kala was the introduction to my real association with the work that Dr Preger was doing, and was to unlock the door that was to reveal to me the answer to many questions.

By this time I had already come to realise that direct contact with the sick and poor in their immediate environment was a special thing involving a wider approach to the situation of the destitute. The patients at Kalighat, in the care of the Missionaries of Charity, formed a final and tragic part of it, but for only a small minority. I wanted to work with and for the living poor. Gradually this was to become a reality that I could not ignore and in time a definite job with Dr Preger emerged, and this took all the energies that I could give it.

I sometimes found it difficult to take everything in. There was so much to assimilate, events taking place in a different culture, in a way of life as different as one could imagine from that in the West which I had left behind. Always there was the engulfing poverty, the continuing shock of which made me feel sickeningly rich amongst the poor. If I gave away everything I possessed, I would still be richer than they could ever be, for I had education, literacy, and health.

The Rain Children

CHAPTER III

JACK PREGER

I believe that the destitute have a right to this kind of help

Dr Jack Preger in his exposition to the Charity Commissioners. This led to the grant of charitable status for the Calcutta Rescue Fund.

CHAPTER III

Jack Preger

WHEN he was not at work Dr Jack Preger lived in the Y, almost as a hermit, occupying a small room on the ground floor. But almost the clock round he was on the teeming streets at the Strand Road flyover area of Calcutta, in the streets that were his practice, under the searing sun by day. Periodically, after he had acquired a dispensary at Middleton Row, he would go back there to write up reports and prescriptions, keeping abreast of the endless paperwork, through the suffocating heat, the load shedding, the monsoon, the early morning and evening. There was no end to it. Over the next seven years the number of his patients grew enormously from about 600 to 6,000. By 1988 he would be seeing most of his patients at Middleton Row.

Over six foot, athletic, he had played hockey for his college. He always moved fast, and with a sense of purpose, simply dressed, often wearing secondhand cottons bequeathed to him by people who had come to know him. Working, he usually carried a khaki canvas bag, and a stethescope.

Direct and honest in his manner, but always courteous, he was liked and respected by everyone. This was not confined to those within the walls of the Y. Outside they knew him too; the street boys, the children, the flower man. There was always someone urgently wanting attention, or waiting to see him.

The first time that I saw the flyover, where Dr Preger was then working, was when he took me there in the early summer of 1981. We went by minibus to Dalhousie Square, and then walked down to the Strand Road and along to the flyover, a massive construction, built to carry ceaseless traffic across to

31

Howrah Bridge. Supported by huge steel reinforced concrete sections, it was home and shelter to hundreds of destitute who live out their lives in its shadows. The word 'flyover' is, of course, primarily the name of the construction itself. However, in this book it is also used in a general sense to refer to the area around it, including the Strand Road and the 'gardens' as they are known: small areas between the roads, known as Flyover North, South, etc., for identification in the records of the patients' whereabouts. All these areas are inhabited by the people. Also, when referring to 'going down to the flyover', one could be thinking of Jagganath Ghat, or under Howrah Bridge, all places which are within walking distance of about fifteen minutes of the flyover, and where patients lived.

Leaving the flyover, we crossed from one of the gardens to another traffic-packed road, at the side of which stretched a line of fractured and broken rickshaws in front of a little row of stalls, where, in the weeks that followed, I used to buy carbolic soap and cut it up into Oxo-sized cubes to give out to the people. On this occasion we did not stop but passed on through a narrow way that led to the opening onto the ghat. This is a large, paved area sloping down to the Hoogly River, where people wash and bath. A small temple stood at right angles to the river; there are always groups of people here, and it is something of an oasis after the thick fumes and dense traffic of the flyover. Above is the enormous and amazing Howrah Bridge leading across to Howrah Station. Its grey steel girders, like a giant meccano construction, throbbed with the life which it carries through the days and nights; it shows as a landmark for miles.

From the temple we retraced our steps and rejoined the road where it passes the brilliant flower market, all orange and white, with marigolds and St Joseph lilies, and a tea stall with its busy custom. The scent from the flowers followed us as we came to the low archway that spans the darkness below Howrah Bridge. As we approached, the cobbled road broadened out for a few yards, and here, using the space to advantage, some destitutes had built lean-to shacks. An asthmatic patient came out from one of these to grasp the doctor by the hand and ask him for more tablets. They talked for a moment before we went under the archway, where blackened stone and concrete contained the gloom, and I felt as though I had moved from technicolour into a world of monochrome black and white.

The cobbled road running under the archway took us along by the wall; it was slippery with crushed garbage and patches of oil.

Here, there was a narrow strip of pavement on the right and along it squatted one or two rice sellers. Here, too, patients often waited to catch the doctor before he went on his visits to the many other people in their shacks, which spread out pathetically along the disused railway platform. The way ahead is divided into three principle parts which comprise, on the far left, the road down which pound lorries and other traffic. Then, in the middle there is a raised platform, and, on the far right, the railway lines. Here the better-off lived. On the platform there are upright supports and girders for the roof. Along here many of the destitute lay. At the base of the sooty girders there were sleeping figures whose pieces of rag and cloth disguised skeletal forms, so that one caught one's breath looking at them, perhaps waiting long seconds before knowing whether the person under the heap of cotton scraps was still alive.

MOST of the people down there knew each other, and they would attract the doctor's attention to any new or serious cases, or accidents. Otherwise the visits followed a pattern that changed little. A group formed around the doctor, materialising from thin air. Saris flapped while babies were carried at the hip by their mothers. The people crowded round, waiting, asking, clutching and holding onto whichever part of them hurt, irritated, or was numb, cut, or burned. These were the walking wounded and, for the most part, one hoped, not too serious cases. But this was hoping too much. Many had TB, leprosy, respiratory or cardiac conditions, and they stayed on their feet until they dropped. When they died, at night very often, it was quite simple; the Hoogly River, the friend of the poor, accepted into its depths the dead. Thus the funeral rites, for which there were no spare rupees, were avoided. Sometimes the dying were found, or looked after by their families. Sometimes they were abandoned. The reasons were usually apparent, the causes also.

SINCE that day when I first saw it, I have seen Jagganath Ghat under different circumstances; in the monsoon, for instance, a black quagmire of filth, with the huts wrecked and lying in the mud or after torrential rain and storms, when tattered pieces of precious polythene had blown off the shacks and clung like prayer flags to overhead girders. I have known Jagganath deserted after raids by the police, following a *lathi* charge. (*Lathis* are the heavy bamboo truncheons used by the police.) They had driven away the poor, the sick, and the children. There were days, in the height of summer, when I wondered whether I could get to the end and back and still have enough energy to walk across Howrah Bridge for a lukewarm drink at the seedy restaurant there, before fighting to get on the homeward bus, which was waiting in the depot outside.

On this first visit Dr Preger led me out on the other side, into the light. By the river wrestlers covered in mud writhed on the ground, practising. A Sadhu sat cross-legged under the shade of his tent, on a rather good mat; he was weak from cholera or gastro-enteritis, as the authorities preferred to call it. The doctor walked quickly between the carts, which were pulled by turbanned men roped together wearing just their simple lungi or dhoti and barefooted. Here, along the cracked and uneven pavements, on the edges of the gutters, their few belongings beside them, always in the heat and under the relentless sun, lived Dr Preger's patients.

I was overwhelmed by what I saw. No one who has seen such poverty can feel the same afterwards. It is there, it exists; therefore one has to do something to help.

But how was I ever going to find again someone I had seen that first day? How was I going to find the same corner, the same hole in the railing where we had slipped through to find the TB patient Hiralal waiting for his drugs and his vitamin tablets? Hiralal's pitch was in one of the flyover gardens, where he lay on a piece of corrugated cardboard, covered with one of the blankets that the doctor arranged to have given out every winter. The garden, which was almost under the flyover, boasted one or two dusty stunted plants and an area of dried ground; a traffic island really, for trams and lorries flowed on each side. It was surrounded by a concrete wall with railings and at one point there was a mound of rubble next to the wall where, later, I used to climb up, to squeeze through the gap in the broken railings, watched usually by the occupants of the crowded trams that stopped there. No doubt they thought me quite mad.

Hiralal was always charming, but he used to grumble if he discovered that his friend, another TB patient down by

34

Jagganath Ghat, had been given an ounce more dried milk or Complan than he had. They carefully compared notes after each of our visits. Both men's names were on the list of TB patients, their X-ray plates carefully stored in the doctor's records.

His room at the Y was packed to capacity with heavy medical books, files and records, drugs and endless lists, and large bottles of gentian violet, which always seemed to be the ones that spilt. Others stood empty, ready for the destitute who did not have bottles, jars, or containers to spare. There were hospital papers, and medical journals. These valuable magazines tended to get 'lost' in the post, which made us curious about the street traders' sources of supply, when seeing the current copy of *The Lancet* for sale on their stalls.

Later, a little lodge at the gate of the presbytery became available, and the doctor was able to store all the medical equipment there, just across the road and at the end of Middleton Row. That was a great help. In due course, by using spare time, we managed to make a card index of each destitute patient, with records of 600 destitute families, their names, and as much medical history as was available. The addresses must be among the most remarkable ever filed: 'the foot of the third lamp-post', 'by central concrete pillar', 'opposite the *thana*' (police station), 'under Howrah Bridge north', 'at foot of steps, southside' and so on. Mother Teresa did not keep records; but we found that their having their name on a record was a start, a beginning for that individual, the nearest perhaps that many would ever come to an official acknowledgement of their identity. Often, people with a complaint, an earache or pain, would go away content to wait when they saw their names had been written down. Then they knew that the doctor, their Dr Jack, would be along to see them again. This card index was started in 1981 and finally brought up to date in 1982, just before I left for England; when I got back again later that year I was to see it enlarged and being added to daily, so that by 1988 it had grown to include about 6,000 patients. It was kept at the little lodge, that has been the base for the Middleton Row street clinic.

Friday was milk-round day in 1981, and I rather dreaded it. Buying all the dried milk made a great hole in the funds available for medicines and hospitals, and everyone on the list, expectant mothers, babies, TB patients and others all needed it desperately. But somehow something always seemed to happen to make it possible to buy the milk for another week. Sometimes it was a donation from one of the interested and understanding people who visited Calcutta and knew of the needs of the people. Sometimes they wanted to help, and asked to go with the doctor, or with me, to see the work. This was always a delicate undertaking.

The people under the flyover knew Jack, and trusted him. They also came to know me, and accepted me because I did things for them, but trust comes gradually, and there is a balance between acceptance on one hand (for one's practical use to someone) and the other unqualified understanding which is love or trust: this is a most precious and valuable reality existing between two people. Simone Weil discussed this subject in one of her books, *Waiting on God,* in a chapter on 'Forms of the implicit love of God'. I am, after all, talking about the question of compassion and its relation to self-respect, self-respect that must be maintained, absolutely intact, by the recipients of compassion, in this case the destitute of Calcutta. 'Generosity and Compassion' she wrote, 'are inseparable, and both have their model in God, that is in creation and in the passion. Christ has taught us that the supernatural love of our neighbour is the exchange of compassion and gratitude which happens in a flash between two beings, one possessing and the other deprived of human personality.' I have often seen examples of this 'flash between two beings'. I have seen it in the patients who surround the doctor when he is with the poor, or when he stops to help a patient unexpectedly. I think this is why, unconciously, he often works alone with these people even when television or newspaper journalists or film crews have come to photograph him at work. The relationship established between him and the person in front of him takes his entire attention, and this attention is creative; it is, as Simone Weil said, a renunciation of self. It is a complete giving of one person to another, and it is because of its entire openness that trust, in its most complete sense, is formed. It creates for the recipients an establishment of themselves in a way that nothing else can.

This is the quality, a quality which never degrades the sufferer, which again and again manifests itself in the work of the doctor. It dictates that such work cannot be hidden, but must be shared, and passed on so that others may be touched by it, as those who meet him are inspired by this selfless man. This is one of the most compelling reasons for writing this book.

Jack Preger is a man who has freed himself, in the sense that we are free when we make a free choice. Men may say we are bound by convention, by a way of life that makes provision for an ordered existence, for sleeping, eating and amusement, for paying bills and associating ourselves with all that we call living. However, there is another choice, and I do not mean the choice of the hippie to opt out from the responsibilities that society imposes, but the choice of using our time in other ways, in action for good. 'If a man has the power to do good, it is sinful for him to leave it undone' (St James, 4:17.). Perhaps that is where the phrase 'do-gooder' comes from, even though as a label it carries an image of some dried-up, self-righteous, individual, who is best perhaps to be avoided.

Tolstoy in *The Kingdom of God is Within* speaks of 'sacrificing outward circumstances for the sake of truth.' The doctor has done this, by leaving, for the most part, the accepted daily life of a British medical practitioner. Certainly he has sacrificed the comforts of home and family life, and the income that goes with a general practice.

The intention of the work of 'Calcutta Rescue', the name which the doctor has given his programme, is that it should be for the living destitute. That is the main point of all his plans and schemes for hospitals that would serve only the destitute, the poorest of the poor, where all medical care would be free, and also the beds, and where, for example, those suffering from TB could be X-rayed without queuing for hours. (Now, this happens only for those who are fortunate enough to be taken to hospital by volunteers, for they are too sick to walk there, and cannot afford the cost of a bus or rickshaw).

The plan would include clinics inside the city, and centres outside, where convalescent patients and those requiring isolation facilities could be sent. Farms and workshops for handicrafts and textiles could be organised, and the products marketed to bring in funds for those engaged in their production. In this way it should be possible to help, in the words of the doctor 'as many as we can, not as few as we can get away with.'

LIVING at exhaust level, breathing in the fumes billowing in the wake of Calcutta's lopsided and drunken-looking buses and lorries, lie the destitute, the needy, the sick, and the dying; and dying they live, not in the way that the world understands the term, but in the sense of still being alive. They survive. Each hour is its own battlefield for it may bring starvation, or fever, or death nearer. Each day brings its repetitive needs; water, food, clothing.

The pigs pick their way through the excrement by the railway lines where parallel to the disused platform are shacks, made of simple posts and pieces of wood, draped around with tattered plastic sheeting and old rags. Stones weigh these remnants down, and there like dogs, the poor crouch down to enter their homes.

The shacks are shelter for their occupants, who are well off compared to the hundreds who lie on filthy rags, or rattan that is stacked up and treasured during the day in dark corners of the structural supports of Howrah Bridge and the flyover. These are brought out at night, of if the owner is sick, are lain on all day and night, to keep a little of the filth of the street from the pitiful cotton rags that serve as clothes for these people.

Despite these appalling conditions people can still smile and take you by the hand, and by laughing they can, perhaps, for a moment escape from their surroundings. But the next moment sees them drawing together scraps of charcoal, which are crushed by hand and made into mounds, mixed with dung and kneaded; they look like little cakes ready for the oven as they are placed on metal platters, waiting for the fire. Later they will fuel the brilliant flames that cook the little fish or vegetables that make the evening meal, while the river washes the last of the bathers with its lapping and polluted movement, its caressing warmth carrying the diseases of the sick through its turbid waters to the early light of the next morning, at the steps of the ghat.

A woman washes the feeding containers in the puddle in the road. She stoops over her work; the passers-by do not disturb her, neither do the great lorries that sweep past, inches from her long brown fingers. She has been doing it for too many years, too many times, and when she is gone the child paddling beside her will do it still. Flower sellers work in the background with their garish orange and red flowers, making garlands for the little temple nearby. They chatter and laugh while their nimble fingers thread the flower heads with great needles and thread. Near them the rice sellers let the rice slip through their hands to top the miniature mountains that are piled before them, as they sit the long day through, cross-legged in the Indian sun.

Abdul Goffur lay immobile beneath a length of cloth, his wife beside him. His condition was poor; he had been sick for many days. He had even been admitted, once, to Kalighat, Mother Teresa's Home for the Dying, and then come back again. But now he had to be taken to hospital, because his X-ray, taken a week before, showed fluid on his right lung. His eyes were dull and questioning, but he knew all the answers to questions that he did not ask. He sat passively in the taxi; a taxi, not a bus, for buses are reluctant to take destitutes, and in any case he was too sick for a bus journey. He was a Moslem who came from Bangladesh, where he had a brother. He was collected early in the morning, to reach the hospital by eight-thirty.

Near where he lay are sleeping babies, their eyes painted with kohl, and their feeding bottles lying tilted beside them, full, not with milk, but with greyish stale barley water, all that the mothers have to give them. Under make-shift mosquito nets, old pieces of net, they slumber in the acrid fumes of the early morning traffic, alone, while their mothers pick rags on a tip, and a crippled child watches them, as a new day starts for the poor, for the maimed, for the sick and dying; and somewhere from the darkness under the bridge is carried above the sound of the traffic the cry of a new born child.

Mohammed Yunus, whose eye is the palest of blue, and shines like the great east window of Chartres Cathedral, sees nothing. The skin around it is puckered and drawn. Indeed, it is hardly recognisable as an eye, but there is in the centre a brilliant pinhead of aquamarine. The other, the right eye, is burned white and scarred. Mohammed Yunus begs, sightless, on Howrah Bridge, a victim of a robbery in which acid was thrown into his eyes. Once he had a shop, now he has nothing. But he is not alone in his misfortune.

SURELY it should be a matter for international concern that Dr Preger's proposals for the establishment of dispensaries for the poor and adult destitutes in the Howrah and Sealdah areas of Calcutta, plans for comprehensive rehabilitation and programmes aimed at overcoming problems related to the destitute, should be put into effect. But in a letter to Dr Preger dated December 26th, 1980, the Assistant Secretary to the

Government of West Bengal wrote 'I am directed to say that your proposal for the establishment of a Home for the Destitute Children and of Dispensaries for the Poor and Adult Destitute at Howrah and Sealdah, has not been accepted by the State Government. The question of giving you permission to acquire land and proceed with the programme does not therefore arise.'

The streets of Calcutta are not paved with gold, they are paved with people, people who have 'surrendered their fundamental right to live', as Jack Preger wrote in an article 'Calcutta's Destitutes', published in the *Tablet* on January 23rd 1980. It is his deep and dedicated belief in this right for these destitute people that has led Dr Preger to serve them and to refuse to abandon them; for, with barely the strength to survive, they have not the mental and physical reserves, the organisation, or even the will to fight for it themselves.

In a letter dated March 3rd, 1983, the doctor sought permission from the Bangladesh Government for the Bangladesh citizens amongst these people to be allowed to return to Bangladesh to be rehabilitated there.

He has also requested the West Bengal Government to allow children, many retarded and spastic among them, together with non-criminal lunatics, to be released from the appalling conditions under which they are kept in Dum Dum Jail. Children in the jail go about half or totally naked, even at the age of ten or twelve years. In February, 1983, the Calcutta *Telegraph* reported that there were 439 children in jail. The *Telegraph* put the blame, or rather the responsibility, on the government and the political masters of the state. Fortunately, the Terre des Hommes organisation in India is raising funds to care for some of the Dum Dum children in a home to be built in Calcutta. But it will take only fifty of them. Some of the non-criminal lunatics have been incarcerated in the jail for years. Anil Khasnobis was admitted to the jail as a lunatic in 1953 at the age of thirty-five. By 1982 he was sixty-four. There are many others, men who have committed no crime but have spent their lives in prison.

Dr Jack Preger has therefore three main continuing concerns: the case for destitute adults and children, the repatriation and rehabilitation of Bangladesh citizens to Bangladesh, and the scandals of the Dattapara camp adoptions and the street kidnappings in Dhaka.

By refusing to abandon these issues Dr Preger faces a possible

40

five year prison sentence, or deportation, for he has failed to obey the spirit of a 'Quit India' order that was served on him by the West Bengal Government, as a result of his involvement in the struggle to end these causes of human misery.

Below the flyover, Calcutta

CHAPTER IV

THE DATTAPARA STORY

... the end is where we start from

T S Eliot

CHAPTER IV

The Dattapara Story

THE story of the adoptions is one that begins in Dattapara refugee camp at Tongi, outside the city of Dacca in the turbulent fledging country of Bangladesh in 1977. It is a blood-drenched country of coups and midnight assassinations, a country that has disposed of four heads of state in twelve years. By 25th March, 1983, Lieutenant General Ershad, Chief Martial Law Administrator, had completed one year of military rule after toppling the elected government of President Sattar.

Until Independence in 1971 Bangladesh had been one of the five provinces of Pakistan, separated from the other four by over 1,000 miles of territory belonging to her neighbour India, of which she was once a part, and from which she was separated by the second partition of Bengal in 1947. The first attempt at partition by the British was under Lord Curzon in 1905, which made Dacca the capital of Eastern Bengal and Assam. This however caused unrest, and was subsequently abandoned.

The Sundarbans, the marshy forests in the Bay of Bengal, habitat of the Royal Bengal Tiger, lie at the margin of the Bay of Bengal, in the delta of the two great rivers, the River Ganges and the Brahmaputra. It is a bay famous for its cyclonic storms and massive tidal waves. The 55,126 square miles of Bangladesh lying at the mercy of these great elements has an enormous density of population, one of the greatest in the world. For every doctor here there are no less than 8,500 people, and a chronic shortage of trained nurses as there are only 1,400 in the whole country. Malaria, TB and cholera are prevalent, and also leprosy. An official source gave the figure as 65,000 cases in 1970. Medical help is mainly available in the towns that doctors prefer to the rural areas, which they tend to avoid.

After natural disasters such as the 1970 tidal wave and cyclone, and the floods in 1972, disease can quickly take on epidemic proportions.

The people who survived the ten month civil war with Pakistan emerged in 1971, after the surrender of the Pakistan army, racked and emotionally drained by it. The consequences of war, with all its acts of inhumanity and terrorisation of civilians, massacres, disease and casualties, was appalling; and the resulting refugees numbered an estimated ten million, most of whom had fled across the border to India. The numbers of those who stayed as displaced persons cannot be guaranteed, but the figure of twenty million has been generally accepted.

That the world came to the aid of Bangladesh is history. The administration faced a formidable task on three fronts: political, economic and social. They appealed for aid, and clearly were thankful for it. Fifty international agencies had responded to this appeal by 1972. That was the year when Dr Jack Preger, answering an appeal for doctors and nurses, came to war-torn Bangladesh, where he remained to work among those suffering millions in refugee camps and clinics, until his deportation by the government in 1979: deportation from a country that he had served so well for seven years.

Many of the refugees who had fled the country returned in 1972, to their destroyed homes and property, to shattered businesses and empty farms, but nevertheless to their new, and independent country, Bangladesh.

THE story of the 'Dattapara Camp Adoptions' is a history of fraud and corruption, appalling in its implications and its suffering. It is the story of how forty-one families were defrauded into parting with their own flesh and blood, their children, by those who purported to be helping them. The story starts in Bangladesh and continues to neighbouring India; it also involves European countries; Denmark, the Netherlands, and others yet to be pinpointed.

'It is urgent that the knowledge of those responsible should be shared. Their destinations should be revealed, and the parents compensated.' These are the words of Dr Preger who, since the first mother hurled herself at his feet imploring his help in his

46

clinic for destitutes in Dacca in 1977, has been campaigning for the disclosure of the whereabouts of the missing children.

Since giving his word to help that mother and many others, considerable efforts have gone on to find the missing children of Dattapara camp. That same year, in 1977, the Directorate of Social Welfare ordered the seizure of Dr Preger's assets. Since that time he has been deported from Bangladesh and ordered to quit India. It seems likely that there is a connection between official hostility to the doctor and the tragedy of the missing children.

The character of a man is what he is, and his reputation is what the world thinks he is; when the two are welded together you have integrity, a very positive force with its own energy, strength, and will. Those who opposed Dr Preger in Bangladesh, must have recognised this as they did all they could to avert the consequences of engaging with him. But they underestimated their opponent, who was to prove David to their Goliath, although the final outcome is not yet known.

IN 1980 a 'Plea for Justice' was sent to the Respected Habihashai Sahib, the Member of Parliament for Patripur, Dhaka. It was from 'The honest and poor women of the Tongi area'.

It appeared from what they swore on oath that the missing children had been collected for an official in a welfare organisation. By using his position, he would have been able to organise the collection of children. In that case it would have been his staff acting on his behalf, who defrauded the parents and took their children, in return for promises that they would be sent to boarding schools provided by the organisation. What is certain is that no such schools existed and that the parents never saw their children again. The tragedy of the loss is written indelibly on the faces of those parents.

Will they ever see them again? It is unlikely.

In the 'Plea for Justice', which I had to read several times to take in, the women alleged they had been threatened and beaten, and feared for their safety.

IN 1983 Dr Preger presented a paper in London on Bengal Vagrants, in which he wrote that further enquiries in Europe in 1982 had shown that six of the missing Dattapara Camp children were reported to have been adopted and a seventh to

47

have died in Holland. The agency responsible for these adoptions stated in 1979 that six of the missing children were in Holland. But subsequently it said none of these children could be found. In 1980 it again changed its mind and found it could account for seven of the children — but this time the information was not made public. Altogether forty-one Dattapara families had now alleged they were defrauded of their children.

After Dr Preger's formal complaint about the missing children, to both the Dutch Authorities and the Bangladesh Government, the Bangladesh Government ordered a full inquiry. But some of the subjects of the inquiry were themselves the investigators of the case and when finally presented, the four-page Government report did not find or indicate any malpractice.

Dr Preger's 'Bengal Vagrants' paper continued: 'In June 1982 the Bangladesh Government imposed additional surveillance on foreign voluntary organisations operating in Bangladesh, and by Ordinance V, The Abandoned Children (Special Provision) Order of 1972 was at the same time repealed. The new Ordinance was accompanied by a Government hand-out stating ''Many children have been taken away from the country with the pretence of being adopted by families under cover of this Order, but in reality they have been criminally used for immoral earnings and gains.'' '

Ordinance V refers to a second scandal prevalent in Dhaka, the kidnapping of children from the streets, to be sold to professional beggars' syndicates, where they face possible amputations, or binding up of limbs, because the income rates increase as the appearance of the child becomes more pitiable. While in Dhaka Dr Preger made a study of these limbs, and looked carefully at the beggars' amputations. He observed a sickeningly consistent similarity in them, as though they had been operated on by someone who had become practised through repetition.

This is one of the possibilities that the deprived parents must think of, as they sit outside their simple huts, with the washing drying in the last of the evening sun. Where is the child who should be sitting with them, playing at the end of the day? Is it now in a brothel? Is it taking part in a blue film or posing for a pornographic photograph?. . . What kind of recompense can be made to compensate these suffering parents?

In Switzerland Madam Renée Bridel is the translator of an American book on international traffic in children. Madame Bridel is a lawyer and also a Swiss delegate for the United Nations in Geneva. Her belief is that the traffic in children is international, and that many thousands from the Third World, including Bangladesh, are sold to other countries where there is a shortage of white children, the United States and Canada amongst them. At present the facts are being monitored and brought up to date. A Dutch reporter for the United Nations was in Calcutta in early March 1982 to see Dr Preger and to collect relevant papers. He was to maintain the search and the investigations in Holland, where in 1981 the Dutch Ministry of Justice had already started their own investigations, having been asked to do so by a Swiss welfare agency. The press has also been active internationally for some considerable time. Help from Interpol has also been sought.

THE Third World is rich in children — and opportunities for acquiring them exist in the right quarters. In Dhaka the processing of all the adoption papers for the whole of Bangladesh, (a country with a population of eighty million) went through the Directorate of Social Welfare. And in Dhaka, in 1982, Mr S. A. Bari, the Social Welfare Minister, was sentenced to three years' imprisonment on charges of corruption.

Poverty is the key to the corruption of the Dattapara Camp scandal. Who could blame those with so much to lose for keeping their mouths shut? Who, for the price of a sari, and facing the loss of their places in the camp, would not choose the easier of two evils: a place in the camp for themselves and their remaining familes, or standing up to their intimidators, who had the power to turn them out?

In 1983 additional surveillance of voluntary organisations was imposed by Ordinance V, by the Bangladesh Government. The Chief Martial Law Administrator of Bangladesh General Ershad is clearly active against corruption, which he has promised to root out, and to stop the traffic in children. But an investigator in Dhaka, seeking the destination of the missing Dattapara children in the adoption records of the Bangladesh Social Welfare Directorate, was told that all the records had been 'locked away'. Dr Preger has requested the opening of these records to be ordered by Ershad. A number of people must know the whereabouts of the children. Thirty-six passports were acquired and thirty-six air-tickets were purchased for them, some by Alan Cheyne, who ran a Danish Adoption Centre in Diamondi and directed the Under-Privileged Educational Programme in Dhaka.

These people, apart from Cheyne who died in 1986, must be made to share their knowledge, as the doctor has said. This may be the most expedient way to begin to rectify, as far as possible, the whole complicated question of the missing children. It is imperative that this be done before more time elapses in the lives of the unfortunate parents and their children.

ALSO in 1983 in London, in July, the Anti-Slavery Society for the Protection of Human Rights celebrated the 150th anniversary of the death of William Wilberforce. The Society, which has supported the doctor in his search for some time, has been working on a report for the United Nations Commission of Human Rights in recent years.

The Anti-Slavery Society holds the names of at least seven children whose whereabouts have been located. The list is also with Terre des Hommes, Lausanne. Mr Peter Davies, then the Director of the Anti-Slavery Society, wrote in a letter to Dr Preger in Janury 1983 that he saw 'no reason why those names should not be sent to the camp', but the Society has put forward the argument that the Dutch families who adopted the 'missing' children in good faith should be protected from the possible repercussions that might occur in the quarter of the real parents and families if their names were given.

The existence of the list of names of those implicated is known to both Swedish and Dutch journalists, and to a British television company in London, which had been engaged in making a film on slavery.

Dr A. K. Barry Rider, Head of a special unit in the Commonwealth Secretariat concerned with combating serious international crime, working in close conjunction with Mr Peter Davies at the Anti-Slavery Society and Dr Preger, has expressed his eagerness to contribute to solving the missing children question, and in putting a stop to the illegal traffic in children.

IN June 1983 a paper became available relating to Dattapara and the trial of a man who had been acquitted of 'Illegal trafficking in Children from Bangladesh'.

The paper was being circulated by none other than Alan Cheyne, who had bought passports for some of the missing children. He had felt it necessary to travel to Geneva in Switzerland to distribute it, whence it found its way to the offices of The Anti-Slavery Society in London.

Cheyne was also having a running vendetta with the editor of the Bangladesh magazine, *Bichitra*. Following a prize-winning article, 'A Gruesome Blackmarket in Asian Children', by Cheryl McCall in the United States journal *The People*, in 1981, *Bichitra* ran an article along similar lines. This resulted in a claim from two parents in the Dattapara Camp that one of the girls in a photograph shown illustrating the pornographic aspects of the affair, was their daughter. The article aimed at highlighting the question of child smuggling in Bangladesh, and pointed to the involvement and implication of Cheyne in the 'heartrending matter of child smuggling'.

At the end of 1986 corroboration of the evidence about the missing children came in the form of eleven affadavits sworn by eleven of their parents.

'THAT these children are "Missing" is good enough reason for them to be found.' These were Dr Preger's words, in June 1983. Today he remains as firmly committed to finding them as ever.

AFTER leaving their hotel one evening at the time of this article, on the way back after dinner and talk with two American journalists from *The People*, who were staying at the Oberoi Grand Hotel and who had come out from the States to cover the Dattapara missing children story, we walked home, at the very edge of the pavement along Chrowringhee to avoid the crowds leaving the cinema. Related to the conversation we had just been having, when Jack had gone through the Dattapara story, clearing points and discussing the present situation, the question of dangers and risks that went with the continuing exposure of the alleged adoptions and the missing children was running through my mind. It would not be out of the question for the doctor to disappear here in this crowded city, especially in some of the areas and places in which he worked. The question of freedom and its relation to one's own degree of commitment seemed relevant. I was thinking aloud, really, while walking quite fast, now that the congestion had eased and the way ahead become clear. On the right of and parallel to the road stretched the shadowy Maidan, its trees and shrubs merging into the night.

How far was one prepared to go? It seemed to me that perfect freedom meant there could be no drawing back at any point, only total commitment. Going the whole way would be sufficient; one should be prepared to accept, even to die, if necessary; only then did you have real freedom. This was a simple statement rather than a question between us. "Oh yes", Jack had answered "of course."

CHAPTER V

A 'QUIT INDIA' ORDER

Quit India

The Government of West Bengal

CHAPTER V

Quit India

ON Saturday, May 30th 1981, President Zia was assinated
in Dacca. I was having coffee in Park Street when I saw
the evening newspaper headlines. I managed to get a paper to
take back to Jack, who still has assets out there including his
clinic, twenty-six bighas of land (about 15 acres) and vehicles
that were taken over by the then Bangladesh Government when
he was deported.

At about this time I wrote in my diary 'The (West Bengal)
Government really wants the doctor to leave West Bengal. The
wearing-down process follows a pattern under which people
generally give up and go. But Jack will never consider leaving
his patients when there is no one else who wishes to take them
on.'

In general, the outside world has no idea what Dr Preger is
up against. For example, an Amercian preacher came to stay,
who was very keen on the work that was being done and felt
that there was no reason why we shouldn't find land and houses
for rehabilitation and clinics and convalescent homes. It was
difficult to convince him that what he was proposing was
virtually impossible; that the government would not allow it
and that even well-established charitable institutions were
struggling. After a while he left for the States somewhat
downhearted and thinking, perhaps, that we were exaggerating
the problems. Now he sends a Christmas card occasionally.

Towards the end of May harassment from the government
increased. A request for a visa to visit Darjeeling was refused.
There was a real clamp down on the doctor's movements.
Also, they were beginning to ask questions about me. What,

they asked, was I doing?

Eventually, as we had expected, a 'Quit India' notice was served, and only three days' grace was allowed. Three days in which to leave India! It seemed probable that Jack would have to go back to the UK, but first he wanted to travel to New Delhi in order to lobby the Minister of Home Affairs in an attempt to secure his position in West Bengal, or to prevail upon Central Government to give directions to that effect. For Central Government had, up to that time, supported the doctor's position, as had the Indian Red Cross. If a meeting in Delhi could strengthen his immediate position it must be undertaken, however difficult it was to spare the time.

It was not the first notice to quit that had been served on Dr Preger. An earlier one had been served in September 1980, when he was given thirty days in which to prepare for his departure, but that time he had managed to get the order indefinitely suspended by the New Delhi Ministry of Home Affairs, who sent a wireless message at the eleventh hour followed by a cable which read 'Reference to our wireless message number 25017/11/90–FI dated 5th November regarding Jack Preger, a British National further representation against quit India order received. Case being reconsidered. In the meantime he may be permitted to remain in the country pending final decision. Detailed letter follows.' It was signed by the New Delhi Ministry of Home Affairs.

The shadow of the West Bengal Government hung heavily over the concentrated activities of the following day, when Jack was engaged in a series of appointments and rounds. At any time the Government could swoop, put him on a plane out of Calcutta, and deport him from India, away from the patients whom he was endeavouring to attend. Meanwhile Derek, our Anglo-Indian helper and my interpreter, was working the clock round getting tickets, fetching prescriptions, running endless errands related to the patients, together with taking detailed instruction from Dr Preger about hospital arrangements for some of them.

The strain on the doctor was great. All his work stood in jeopardy; for if he was arrested there was no one to take on the care of his people. There were other considerations, such as his belongings; all the medical books and equipment, records and files. Some of his things would need to be sent back to the UK, others stored. The uncertainties of the situation meant that

plans had to be made carefully, without confusion. To cover
one contingency Jack wrote a brief note assigning the contents
of his small and overcrowded room to my care, and signed it in
an unusually large hand. The need to travel to Delhi was
becoming greater, for as the hours passed it became clearer that
Central Government would have to be consulted, and it was a
possibility that they would suggest leaving India as a way of
overcoming the 'Quit India' notice, which was the immediate
problem for Jack. So there was the packing, too. What should
be taken, and what left? It was unlikely tht he would be allowed
to return straight to Calcutta from Delhi, so Jack had also to be
prepared to go out of the country to Nepal.

Among all those decisions and arrangements, we went down
to the flyover to take what might prove to be my last
photographs of the flyover people; some of those photographs
now illustrate this book.

At about lunch-time, when we went back to the Y, the
Security Police called. I thought they were going to arrest Jack
before he could get to Delhi; however they went away and came
back later with a letter for Jack which stated that he would not
get the extension which he had applied for. Things were not
improving. Previously the Deputy Commissioner of Security
Police had arranged that he and Jack would go the next day
together to see Shri A. K. Mukerjee, Deputy Secretary of the
West Bengal Government, but now Jack was afraid he would
withdraw that offer, and, in the event the meeting did not take
place.

PEOPLE were being very kind and supportive in the
circumstances. One friend looked after all my odd valuables, air
ticket, presents for home, letters, etc., and the important
patients records, and papers. Mrs Moffat, the secretary at the
Y, was paid up so she would keep my room for another month
for me. Whatever was needed for Delhi was packed, together
with thicker clothes for Nepal if need be. Before leaving for
Howrah Station Derek had returned from his last errands to
come with us to the train, and to take final instructions from
Jack, after a speedy last round of some sick patients at Jaganath
Ghat.

Finally, at the end Jack did not know what to say. Who could
tell at that point what the outcome would be? I thought him
remarkable to stand out against so many odds, as did everyone

57

who knew the inside story.

The train to Delhi was a good one and we were able to eat on it. Jack was wrestling with a heavy cold and was very tired, which was not surprising. We heard that Delhi was in the grip of a pre-monsoon heat wave, but at least there were no mosquitoes in the city as the streets were sprayed regularly with a deterrent; also the electricity supply there was good, with an absence of the dreaded load shedding.

IN New Delhi there was a great deal to be done. Firstly, there were appointments to be made. The Member of Parliament whom Jack needed to see most of all was about to leave for Shrinigar. However, after seemingly endless telephone calls an appointment with him was arranged. There was also the Red Cross to see, then various newspapers, the Ford Foundation and many other people. I got a personal appointment with the Apostolic Delegation which took up one entire afternoon but was not productive. The Apostolic Delegation said that they could not help in any way, and that they had their own difficulties. They did suggest that working in the south of India would be easier, and that West Bengal was known to be fraught with problems.

Delhi is an easy city to get around in but of course, as a capital city, it is more expensive than Calcutta. There are motorcabs, a kind of motor cycle rickshaw which are very quick, and all the Delegations and Embassies are near one another which was a help. There were endless letters to be sent off and articles for the press to be written. Sandwiched between all this activity we tried to see a bit of the city of both Old and New Delhi which is rich in history and in superb buildings. The Red Fort overlooking the river Jammu was impressive, with its fine red sandstone walls glowing in the sun. Built centuries ago by the Mughal Emperor Shah Jahan, within its massive walls are contained many treasures.

The historical aspects of Delhi, superb as they were, to me seemed overshadowed by modern history; by Independence and Gandhi and Nehru; and by modern architecture of the new capital. Calcutta was the capital of India until 1911 when King George V, the first British sovereign to visit India, announced that Delhi was to be the new capital.

There on Rasina Hill, in a spatial setting with commanding views down the great vista to India Gate, stand the buildings of both the North and South Secretariats. They house the government of the sub-continent in not less than a thousand rooms — outside many of which the doctor was destined to spend many hours waiting for interviews, waiting to discuss his case, waiting on the whim of officials. . .

I did not know then that I would return here the following year, alone, when I would travel back from England via Afghanistan and Delhi, and would be once more petitioning the government: that was still in the future. Now, in the heat of pre-monsoon Delhi, the days were taken up with walking, waiting, and writing, the outcome as uncertain as ever.

The Indian Red Cross interview with the doctor had been favourable; they were happy for him to work in India, only too pleased. Finally, there was an indication of the next move by the Government. The verdict was that it would be advisable for the doctor to leave India, go to Nepal, and then re-enter India, after a few days. They also said that they were happy for him to work in India, but that it might be necessary for him to work outside the State of West Bengal. This confirmed the Apostolic Delegation's line. So now there were visas to get at the Nepalese Embassy, and more tickets for another train, this time to the border.

DELHI had been rewarding for me. I was able to see the Gandhi National Museum, and to study for one whole day all the things there, including Gandhi's books, etc. While the doctor was lobbying M.P.s I also visited Nehru's house, which is open to the public as a museum. I liked especially a carving of Gandhi that was in the museum, an almost Christlike figure, and one that later inspired a letter-heading that I was to design for the Calcutta Rescue Fund, the charity that came into being for the relief of the pavement dwellers.

One picture that I found satisfying in the Gandhi Museum was 'The Three Seer's of Ages' (sic). This portrayed a landscape packed with a dense population and through it, on what appeared to be an elevated path amongst them, came the figures of Buddha, Christ, and Gandhi, in that order. They were walking the path to the distant horizon, over the sea and to a great sun, circle of light — eternity.

THE train journey to the Nepalese border was quite different from any other I have ever undertaken. Certainly we knew it

59

was going to be long, starting in the early morning from New Delhi and going to Raxual, whence we would travel by government bus to Katmandu. The monsoon had started. It was going to be difficult to see the Himalayas at all; it would be cloudy and very wet, and the roads would be poor.

First we had to get to Raxaul by rail. The people travelling were a colourful lot, among them a couple with a tree, or rather a young sapling, that took up most of my legitimate leg space, and a hippie couple. The girl never spoke, but left her seat from time to time to return with cold cream all over her face, that gradually vanished; vanishing cream perhaps? There were meals on the customary metal plates, trays really, with built-in bowls, full of rice and curry. We did not go hungry. At the stations there were little terracotta bowls with tea and we had fruit. Jack read *The Lancet* as if he was on the 9.30 am to Paddington, and I had a huge Fulton Sheen paperback that I have never to this day finished, with a Salvador Dali cover. Our red thermos flask was full of water and slung up on the hook, and I had also brought limes.

Gradually the people thinned out, and on the last stages of the journey at about 11 p.m. there was no one left in our compartment, except three youths. At one station light from a torch shone in through the windows. "What is it?" I asked.

It was an official in uniform white trousers, black jacket, and dark rimmed glasses.

"It's not you," came the reply. "It's those three."

Immediately afterwards he sent along three armed guards, who came clattering in with their rifles and sent the youths out of the carriage. "We don't want you to be robbed."

The guards stayed with us from then on for sometime. The guard of the train was to let us know when we reached Raxaul at 3.30 in the morning, as we were afraid that we would be asleep. At one point in the journey, at about 1.00 a.m., the armed guard who was sitting at my head as I slept on the seat, woke me. Jack was fast asleep opposite. The guard gestured that they were getting out now and I must lock the door after them, and hide my face. It took me a few moments to realise the implications as I was still half asleep: we were to be alone in this part of the train — our own and the next compartment, together with the bit of corridor — which had, in all, two doors and many windows.

At the stop the guards barred the way with their rifles, and everyone getting in had to board other parts of the train. Then, as they jumped off the footplate down into the darkness below I locked the door behind them.

I was alone with the luggage and Jack who, relaxed at last in the knowledge that we would be woken at Raxaul, was asleep on the bench seat.

Someone stared in through the bars of the window and, remembering my instructions, I wrapped my scarf around my face, dacoit fashion, and sat down. The train moved slowly out from the station, leaving peering faces and the receding platform behind.

I must have fallen asleep too, for the next thing I remember was arriving at the station, and then everything happening together. The guard of the train came in, Jack got the things down and onto the platform; a rickshaw man came forward out of the night, loaded up our things, and we were off again — out into the fresh air, inside the Indian border, but with Nepal virtually just across the road.

AFTER only one day to recover from the marathon train journey we had to leave Raxaul the following morning, again very early at about 4.00 a.m., again in a rickshaw, with all our baggage stacked up, including the red thermos flask which now seemed to leak. The border was five kilometres away.

Then we had to get tickets for further transport, by a government bus that was to take us up to Katmandu for 76 rupees, less than £4.00, each. It was a nine-hour journey through hills of up to about 3,000 metres, or about 9,000 feet. The bus was waiting and we had to rush to catch it, as at the border it had taken us some time to clear immigration; but then we were through, Jack thereby fulfilling his order to 'Quit India', in the way suggested by Delhi.

There was just time to fetch quickly some scalding lemon tea, before once again it was on, on.

The early morning was incredible, for high in the clouds, superb, with the sun shining on their summits, were the Himalayas. We couldn't stop looking at them, for we knew that within the hour they would have vanished, blotted out by rain, until the next dawn. I wished so much that it was not the monsoon, and that it would be possible to look at them all the time; but to have seen them at all was a great experience.

The bus journey was tiring, the roads bad. We stopped in a

village that was terribly poor, with nothing but simple dwellings, and people staring at us. Later, higher up in the hills, the bus stopped again for more passengers. At one stop I got out because my legs were stiff, and walked along the road a little, then hurried back as the bus driver was hooting. When I returned to my place I realised that I had managed to collect leeches on my legs. They were hooked into me and Jack had to get them off.

At last we reached the top of the terraced hills, where every inch was planted. Finally, we could see down to the valley to Katmandu, almost another world.

There were to be only two or three days in Katmandu, as Jack had an appointment with a politician in Calcutta on the 20th July. So we would have to see then what would happen at the border, and if they would let him back.

It was St Swithin's Day, and there was no doubt about the monsoon. We walked, however, as it was so marvellous to be able to move about after sitting still during all the travelling. There were the most wonderful temples, Hindu Temples, pagodas dedicated to Shiva, Buddhist monks, a Living Goddess who was in fact a child, and pilgrims everywhere, prostrating themselves for miles along the way, measuring their own length on the ground. . . before reaching the *stupa* that was their goal, a Buddhist dome-shaped shrine. Katmandu was far more than the guidebook said, and it is impossible to describe it here; I can only say that I could hardly believe it.

The Buddhist monks at The Great Temple were guardians of the sacred fire and they had superb musical instruments; the sound from their horns, which rested on little trolleys for mobility, echoed across the valley. There were drums also, and gongs. Many stone steps leading up to Swayambhunath were fringed with monkeys, and from the terraces I could see the town but, sadly, because of the monsoon, not the mountains. It is a town packed with fantastic architecture, shops and stalls, street markets, Tibetan jewellery, women with earrings down the outer side of their ears, mountaineering equipment shops, trekking information, people, and everywhere intricate carving and designs that confuse you in their variety among statues and monuments.

THE journey back to Calcutta from Katmandu started at 3.30 in the morning, again in a bus. All the luggage was thrown on top and by now my case was getting into bad shape. The route was to Kakavita, near Siliguri, whch would take about sixteen hours. Then, after crossing the border, there would be another bus to Calcutta. It was a daunting prospect, but inexpensive. Also, it was frustrating to pass points marked up as 'Everest View' with a vantage point and telescope; but then we were hardly tourists!

The hostel, where the bus finally stopped, was a tiny place, exceedingly simple. The rooms were no bigger than a railway compartment, and for the first time I felt, no doubt due to near exhaustion, a moment of despairing anger at the mud outside and the lack of comfort within. It was temporary, and it passed after food and then a shower by the light of a single candle, that was stuck on to a tiny ledge and almost blown out by the irregular gushes of water.

THE next day another rickshaw was loaded up and we walked beside it to the Nepalese border point, where the border guards stamped us out of Nepal. Then, with the luggage still in our rickshaw, we walked over the empty flat area to the Indian frontier post. The guard took our passports, and Jack followed him into the tent. I waited with the rickshaw man and the luggage. . . Nothing happened. I could see them talking inside. Another guard looked me up and down. I ignored him. Then Jack came out and told the rickshaw man to stay there and we both went back inside. The officials had gone to get someone 'in authority'. I thought 'This is it; they are not letting us back'. The senior man came slowly in, putting on his jacket. We needed a permit, he said. We would have to go to Darjeeling to get one although the permit office would be closed to-day as by now it was Sunday morning. We protested; we were not staying, merely passing through the Darjeeling area, and the doctor had an appointment the following day, an important one, so he had to get back. The man said we could not go through, then suddenly announced that he could not stop us if we did, but that he could not stamp us in. He gave us back our passports. We went on, and crossed. Then we took another bus into Siliguri; we were looking forward to getting a meal, and what we hoped would be our last booking, for two places on the overnight bus to Calcutta.

THE bus did not go well at all, and after four hours on the

Calcutta run it broke down. Everyone on it stormed and shouted at the driver, wanting their money back, till 4 o'clock in the morning, when they all melted away into the night. We were told that a relief bus had been sent for, but it never arrived. At dawn, struggling with the luggage, we set out for the local bus stop and waited for yet another bus that took us back to Siliguri where, after fierce argument, the bus people gave us new tickets for the evening bus. In that, packed to capacity, with Hindi music blaring over the loudspeaker system and my ankles swollen by the heat and travelling, we eventually made it back to Calcutta.

In Calcutta Jack was given a forty-eight-hour extension to his 'Quit India' notice. "But really", he said, "they would have preferred to arrest me."

CHAPTER VI

THE CASE OF DR JACK PREGER

Be truthful, gentle and fearless

M Gandhi

CHAPTER VI

The Case of Dr Jack Preger

EIGHT days later, on 26th July, I had just changed for dinner when Ali, the waiter, knocked on my door.

"Dr Jack," he said, "call you. . . big car with wire. . . " His fingers traced criss-crosses in the air. I knew exactly what he meant, and realised why Jack had been out so long that afternoon. What we had both feared and expected had happened: he had been arrested.

I rushed down the stairs, Ali at my heels. Outside the lights of the street were reflected in the shiny pavement, and the police van stood on the opposite side of the road, as still as the hot night. I looked through the back window grill, but there was no one inside. The driver in the front pointed at the Y, indicating that they were still there. I rushed back across the road and re-entered the Y. His room was full of police, with Jack standing head and shoulders above them all.

"They are arresting me," he said. "Take my keys and my watch."

The police seemed to be all round us. There were four or five of them overflowing from the small room into the passageway. Jack took off his watch and handed it to me. Then everyone went out and he locked the door, handing me the keys. Together we left the building, which was quiet, as people were in their rooms getting ready for dinner.

I asked the police where they were taking the doctor.

"To Lalbazar lock-up," they said. "Tomorrow he'll be up before the magistrate at twelve noon."

They put him in the van; Jack saluted and I saluted back.

"Bonne chance," I said. "I'll go directly to the British High Commission."

For a moment events had the air of musical comedy. Then the police van drove off. The show was over, there was a dark empty street, and reality. An English doctor working for the poor and helpless had been taken away, not only from his place of residence but from those destitute people, to whom he had given years of devoted service both in Bangladesh and in India.

THE story of this chapter is one of intrigues involving jails and courts, police commissioners, public prosecutors and Security Control, solicitors and barristers, seedy lawyers in dusty greenish-black jackets, and of packed courtrooms, prisoners roped together, and bribery and corruption played out in intolerable heat.

People wait for hours by the jail for the chance of a fleeting glimpse into a passing police truck and the sight of a relative or friend. And all this goes on in a so-called democracy.

Gandhi said, when referring to non-violence, 'It is possible for a single individual to defy the whole weight of an unjust empire to save his honour, his religion, his soul.' Was Jack Preger to be such an individual? Could he defy the weight of the Government of West Bengal, not in order to save his soul or his honour, but to preserve his position as a doctor, so that he could go on helping the poor in Calcutta?

The Government of West Bengal, who did not wish him to remain, were holding him under the Foreigners Act, Section 14. He had been served with a notice to quit, and this, they held, he had violated by not leaving India.

The matter was as simple as this. Central Government alone, under the Foreigners Act, had the authority to implement, or issue this notice, but they had not done so. Nevertheless, Jack was to spend the next eight days in Alipore Special Jail in Calcutta.

Although his whereabouts were well known to the authorities it took me over sixteen hours to discover where he was being held.

The day after his arrest I telephoned Lalbazar Jail, to enquire if the doctor had passed a good night, if he was all right, or needed anything. I also asked them to tell me at what court house he was to appear before the magistrate at noon.

68

The answer was that they did not have a prisoner of that name. I said I was told by the police that he was to spend the night there. Then they said, "Yes, we do have him; he's English," but if I wanted to know where he was to be brought before the magistrate I must go to see Security Control, who would be able to tell me.

This happened on the Prince of Wales' wedding day. The night before, after the police had driven Jack off, I had gone to the British High Commission in the first taxi I could get, to register the fact that a British National had been arrested, and was in Lalbazar. The guards at the BHC telephoned the Second Secretary, Mr Bruce, for me. My bag was searched for bombs, or whatever guards search for, and then I was admitted, and spoke to the Second Secretary on the telephone from the Gatehouse. Because of Prince Charles' wedding the next day, I was told, the High Commission was closed, and they could do nothing.

I protested that they must do something; they should at least be present at the magistrates' court. I told them that Jack had been assured by the Joint Secretary of Home Affairs in Delhi that he could continue his work in India. Finally Mr Bruce said that he would telephone me at the Y in the morning.

The Second Secretary kept his promise and telephoned at ten the next morning. He reiterated what he had said the night before. He advised me to get a lawyer, which I had already done, and said that they would be in touch after the royal wedding. He rang off.

Meanwhile, I still did not know at which magistrate's court Jack was to appear, so I hurried to the office of Security Control, where I asked to see Inspector Ratan Bhattacharjee. He was not in. I waited. I was concerned about the time. Already it was 10.30 and I had somehow got to find a solicitor who had to get to the right court by noon.

When the Inspector arrived we left the dusty marble hall and plastic covered seats where I had been waiting, for an even dustier office. He asked me what I wanted and I explained that I wished to know the magistrate's court at which Dr Preger was to appear that same morning.

"I have his file," the Inspector replied, and snapped his fingers. An office boy held out a brown folder; the pages inside slipped loosely as the Inspector waved it away again.

"He will appear at Bankshall Court at 11.00 a.m. today, in Calcutta."

I asked him to be kind enough to write it down for me so that I could give it to the solicitor. He obliged.

"May I use your telephone, to ring it through?"

He got up and led me through to another office, where I was given a seat and a telephone, "For the Memsahib to be comfortable," and then he listened as I rang the solicitor and read off the address I had just been given. Then I left for the Court.

Bankshall Court was in a red brick building. The whole place was alive with people, lawyers, clerks. I went upstairs to the courtroom where the case would be heard. The solicitor had arrived; we talked. He said that there should be no difficulty in arranging for a release on bail, and that he would move on that. Then we waited, but Jack did not arrive; other prisoners did. Meanwhile I was informed that if I wished to speak to the prisoner out of the cage (as they called it) I would have to pay 300 rupees. I said I could not do that, and that I would have to speak to him in the cage. They said that would be almost impossible. (These suggestions came from one of the clerks of the court.) I continued to wait. It was possible, they said, that the case could be heard in another courtroom. For thirty rupees I could have two men posted at the other two courts. The thought of missing the case for the want of thirty rupees was too much and I succumbed to the offer.

The solicitor had meanwhile left to attend to some urgent business, but now returned. By this time I realised that something was badly wrong. I found a telephone in the barristers clerks' office, and telephoned the British High Commission. I told them that I was concerned that Dr Preger had not appeared in the court as Security Control had told me he would, and that his whereabouts was not known to me. They put me through to Security Control (I have never quite fathomed how) where I spoke to an officer who was just coming off duty. By now it was 4 p.m. "Dr Preger," he said, "is at Alipore Magistrates Court, and has been there all day!"

I felt that I had been deliberately misled. The magistrates would finish sitting at 4.30 p.m. and I would never get there in time to get him released that day.

I left the building, taking the solicitor with me. The traffic was streaming in all directions, there was no taxi and I felt sick with apprehension. On top of that, in the search for a taxi I had lost sight of the solicitor. However he re-appeared with a cab

70

Howrah Bridge

Hoogly River

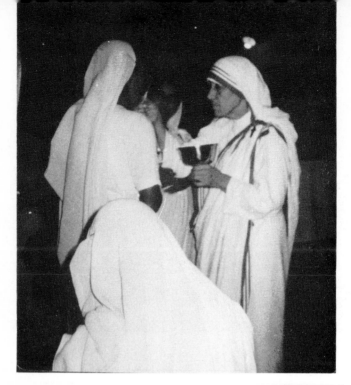

Mother Teresa giving the Sacrament

On the roof at Kalighat

Armenian Ghat

A fortune-teller's parrot

The author with Makul and her father

Dr Jack Preger at work

A leper under the flyover

Pipe-dwellers in Bangladesh

Dr Preger with patients

Exhausted

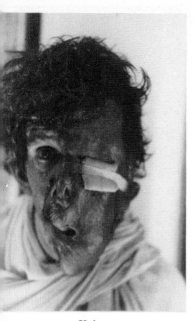

Kala

Undercover in the rain

Breakfast

A patient of Dr Preger's

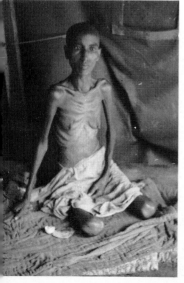

Where the doctor treats patients at Middleton Row

*Invalid carriage provided by the
Calcutta Rescue Fund*

and we were able to get away from Bankshall Court.

Later it turned out that in fact Dr Preger's case should have been heard before the magistrate at the Bankshall Street Court.

Alipore Court was away from the rushing traffic, in a better part of Calcutta. The court-house was a dirty white, and the Police Inspector's office was tiny. I demanded to see the doctor. I told the Inspector that I felt I had been deliberately misled as to his whereabouts that day. They said it was too late to arrange bail, but that I could see him.

At first I could only see, through the bars, a mass of men of all ages, all Indians. Beside me the warder held a great key. Then in the middle of them all, as someone called out "Memsahib" and pointed, I saw him, waving and smiling. The cell door swung heavily open and they let him out, and indicated a bench where we were able to sit. We talked, and I explained the situation, told him the news, and asked him what it was like.

"They beat them up," he said. "One has just had an epileptic fit, and they wouldn't let him out; but it's all right now."

When time was up I went back to the office. A few minutes later the prisoners were herded into a police truck to go to Alipore Special Jail.

That evening I went to see Professor Bose, a member of the Legislative Assembly. He knew an MP in Delhi, a member of the Indian Red Cross, who had told him how much the doctor could do if he worked for them in India. Professor Bose said he would be happy to talk to Mr Sen Gupta (West Bengal Home Secretary) and to Mr Mukerjee (Secretary, Home Affairs) about Dr Preger. He wanted to be kept in the picture, also he would like a letter from the Joint Secretary for Home Affairs in Delhi, stating that they were happy for Dr Preger to work in India.

The next morning I went to see Mr Bruce at the British High Commission. The Royal Wedding was over, but I will not forget it, nor the date and day I spent in an Indian court and jail.

The Second Secretary said he would visit Jack that afternoon. We talked for a while. I said I wanted Jack's release, bail, and permission for him to go to Delhi. I complained at being deliberately misled by Security Control the day before, and asked him to verify and confirm Jack's whereabouts. This he did. Jack was in Alipore Special Jail. It took him half an hour to find it out, "And," he said, "it was not easy."

Next I went to the Legislative Assembly, and was just about to go in when a car stopped, and Professor Bose leaned out of the window. I had almost missed him. It was late. We talked in the car. "Come and see me tonight, at home." I agreed and got out. Once again I looked for a taxi, for I had to go to see a politican who also knew Dr Preger and the Red Cross MP.

The place was well out of the centre of Calcutta, and I had to be back at the jail by 3.30 p.m. in order to meet someone from the British High Commission there. It was hot, and I waited on the verandah of the MP's house, set in a pleasant shady little village. Apparently the MP was having lunch. Suddenly he appeared, and enquired what could he do for me. When I explained he got out Jack's file, and went through it, handing out papers and certificates that would help him. Then he wrote a letter for me to take to Professor Bose, asking him to do all he could. There was half an hour left in which to get back to the jail. It was an hour's journey by mini bus, so I looked again for the taxi that I always seemed to need, and half an hour later walked up to the prison gate. The BHC car was parked outside, its flag furled and masked.

The armed guard unlocked the prison gate, carefully pointing out that I might hit my head if I did not lower it as I entered (never once in all the times that I visited Alipore Special Jail did they fail to point this out!). Then we went in, accompanied by one of the guards. They wore khaki and carried guns. We went up a short flight of stairs to the jailor's office.

Mr Bruce was there, as I knew already, so was Jack, and there were others. We talked, it was cheerful, and there was a certain amount of humour. We must move for bail. It was suggested that as the doctor had not in fact chosen a solicitor himself he should now do so. Mr Gupta, the jailor, suggested a Mr Bhattarcharjee, who was available at Alipore Court. He would put us in touch with him, and he could visit the doctor, who agreed to this.

When Mr Bruce left we were allowed to talk together for a while, until I had to leave to go to court, to meet the solicitor. It was the same place that I had been to the day before, but this time I went to a little wooden open stand. There were dozens of these stands from which solicitors' clerks did their work. From

72

this 'chicken coop', as we called it, much of this continuing story took place.

It was at this place that a day or so later, Mr Bhattarcharjee asked me for 500 rupees for the Public Prosecutor which, after considerable doubts, I paid him on the morning of August 4th, 1981. (This matter was later referred to the Indian Law Society because of the seeming irregularity of the payment.)

The chicken coops were between the various court buildings, and a constant flow of people went past, including twice a day a long row of prisoners, roped together, going to and from the court. They were confined to a room there, next to the court, the heat and stench from which pervaded the courtroom.

The clerk found Mr Bhattarcharjee and we told him that the jailor Mr Gupta had recommended him, and asked him to see Dr Preger and to move for bail as quickly as possible.

He said he would return to the jail with me, and asked me to wait for a while, which I did; and then I walked back to the prison, about eight minutes away from the court, with him. The prison building itself was rather Mexican-looking, with first the high wall, and then the gates of heavy-duty netting with one square that opened, to let visitors into a large open courtyard with railings on the right, behind which were buildings used by the guards. The entrance to the jail was arched, like Traitors' Gate, and over it on a castellated brick pyramid flew the flag of India. This was lowered each evening, when the guard stood to attention and presented arms.

It was too late for me to see the doctor again, but I saw Mr Gupta with Bhattarcharjee and discussed the case. Gupta said he was embarrassed at having the doctor in his jail, among murderers and other criminals, and that he should be out on bail; that, after all he was a good man, Dr Jack, who worked for the poor. I asked him if I could leave the Calcutta *Statesman* for Jack to read; he said I need not bother; he would give him his own, when he saw him later. I handed over some anti-malaria tablets together with some anti-mosquito cream because Europeans are liable to get malaria easily, and the doctor was on a course of tablets. These Mr Gupta accepted and said they would be passed on to Jack.

Then different aspects of the case were talked over, and tea arrived. After that I arranged to be in the court the next day, the solicitor was set to work on the 'Prayer to the Magistrate', and I was told that as there was to be an eclipse of the sun next morning the court would not sit until noon.

The heat of the day over, I walked back to the top of the road, to the bus stop by the Alipore Zoo, where it was almost countrified, with ducks flying overhead and gardens.

Many thoughts went through my mind. I thought of the night of the storm, in the monsoon earlier this year, when floods had wrecked the shacks and poverty-stricken areas where the poor lived, and how the doctor had asked the Mother Teresa's Sisters of Charity to help, by taking over the area he was working in, and they had refused. The Sisters said "Ask the Brothers," and the Brothers said "Ask the Sisters".

The Lutherans did not want to assist in running the programme. They said that they only helped West Bengalis and that there were many people not from West Bengal among the poor there. The fourth organisation that Dr Preger had approached on that occasion was the Salvation Army who said that they would let him know, but never did.

When I reached the Zoo, I thought of the analogy of the prison bars behind which I had left Jack and the beautiful creatures confined there.

I thought of the money I had paid to the solicitor, allegedly for the Public Prosecutor; of the 300 Rupees I had been asked for to talk to a prisoner out of the cage in Bankshall Court; and of all the other petty bribes along the line, for instance in getting a paper or document stamped before the magistrate rose at 4.30 p.m. The Release paper had to be signed by the magistrate, taken back to the jail before the prisoners were locked up for the night, countersigned by the jailor, and returned to the magistrate before he rose, which was a physical impossibility. It meant that a prisoner who had been released on bail could not get out that day if his case came up in the afternoon. And there were the atrocious conditions in the prisoners' cell: the stifling heat and overcrowding. The occupants of the Zoo cages were better off, I thought.

Clearly, each day now had a pattern to it; one of waiting, interspersed with great activity.

The solicitor had prepared a Prayer to the Magistrate and we had copies of all the relevant papers and certificates from the Indian Red Cross, from Mother Teresa, and from others, praising the doctor's work in India and Bangladesh.

The solicitor's main defence was that the Foreigners Act said that Central Government alone could authorise the extradition

74

of a foreigner, and this authority had not been given, and also that in a wireless message sent to Dr Preger in November 1981, Delhi said that the matter was 'Pending Further Decision'. That further decision had never been made, and there the case should have rested.

As I waited for the bus I realised that I would again have to go to see Professor Bose, whom I had now seen on several occasions. He now suggested that a letter should be obtained from the British High Commission stating that they would take responsibility for Dr Preger while he visited Delhi, which was one of the reasons that he wanted to be released on bail. He assured me that when the letter had been read by Mr Sen Gupta the West Bengal Home Secretary, and Mr Mukerjee the Deputy Secretary for Home Affairs, he would talk to them again, but that meanwhile I should get the letter.

All this took place after a great storm that evening, the water lying across the road in enormous floods in front of Professor Bose's house and my taxi driver reluctant to take me through them. I was glad to be back in central Calcutta by the end of the day.

Because of the total eclipse of the sun and the court sitting late, Jack's case was not heard the next day. It was now due to come up again on the Saturday. Meanwhile, while there was time, I went to the British High Commission.

The gates were locked, but the security guard knew me, and after the usual search I was let in. There was no one about, only the security officer and he, I was told, was asleep. It was 9.30 a.m. I asked to speak to the duty officer but he was not in; I asked for the Deputy Commissioner and he also was not there. I said that the security officer must be woken as I had to speak to the officer in charge. After a while the security officer came out onto his balcony to shake what I took to be his sleeping bag. I thought of the court that started at 10 a.m. and how I had left a message the previous evening, and how the security officer had promised to telephone me that morning. As I went up the stairs leading to his quarters, he came slowly down to meet me, and agreed to telephone the duty officer and Mr Bruce.

I waited. The duty officer arrived and I related the case to him. He was kindly. He said he would telephone the Deputy Commissioner, and drafted the letter which was required.

Again I waited, the guards grouped outside the door of the room we were in. They had been following the case over the last few days and one of them asked how the doctor was getting on. "Still inside," I said, "And it's high time they got him out."

The duty officer returned, the draft in his hand. "I have spoken to the District Commissioner," he said. "The Second Secretary is the only one who can write this letter; he is playing golf at the Tolleygunge Club but he is expecting you."

The taxi swept into the gravelled drive, and the lawns of the Club were green and pleasant, where people were drinking or playing golf. I asked for Mr Bruce and he came up in his impeccable white shorts, carrying a multi-coloured golfing umbrella. I asked if he would be kind enough to write a letter that would be instrumental in helping to get Jack out of the prison, and if he could return there with me.

He was hesitant. I said if he did not write it, then one could argue that a British National was being held in an Indian jail by the British High Commission.

"What do you want me to say?" he asked.

So on the bar of the Tolleygunge Club he wrote the letter that had been suggested by Professor Bose and which on my return to Alipore Special Jail I showed first to the jailor, and then to the doctor, when I was able to see him.

Finally I left to see the Home Secretary, an appointment having been telephoned through from the prison to the Secretary for Home Affairs at the Writers' Buildings in Dalhousie Square. When I arrived I was taken up to the second floor along miles of passageway and into the Home Secretary's room. Briefly, he looked at the letter and asked me to follow him; we passed several guards sitting in the long corridor, which reminded me of the Gallerie des Glaces at Versailles, without the mirrors, and into a small office, dominated by a large desk. The room was full of men who were hostile, but polite, and painstakingly slow. They knew that the court was in session and that the letter was needed there. Deputy Secretary Mukerjee said that he would not interfere with justice, and another official said that Dr Preger's case was an offence under the Foreigners Act and only the magistrate could decide. I explained that Professor Bose of the Legislative Assembly, and the jailor (Mr Gupta) had told me it was possible for the case to be dropped, and that was what I was asking for.

Mukerjee said that the best thing for me to do was to get back to the court with the letter, before it was too late. By now it was mid-afternoon. I asked if he would telephone through and tell them at the court of the letter and its contents or a whole week-end would pass before something could be done. He slowly reached for the phone, and as had been the case all through the affair, it did not work. I asked if I could telephone the jailor, Gupta, who would send a runner to the solicitor. "Yes," he said. By now they were all watching me, wanting me to panic, to be upset; deliberately I dialled the number, but it did not work. "Thank you, gentlemen," I said, and left the room.

By the time I got back to Alipore, needless to say, it was too late and the case was postponed again. We would have to wait. Mr Gupta had told me earlier that the following day was the Moslem feast of Eid. It would be a good day for them in the prison as food and other things for the prisoners could be handed in. Until then I had thought each day would see Jack's release, but now it was certain that it would not be before Monday at the earliest, so I went to the market on the way home and bought things for the next day, and got out some books, and made up a bundle for him. All that was missing was the proverbial cake, with a file in it.

On Sunday, after carefully checking through it, the jailor gave the bundle to Jack. He suggested that I telephone the Commissioner of Police and make an appointment with him to ask for the case to be dropped. I did this and an interview was arranged for the next day at noon.

Our meeting was brief. I pointed out yet again that under the 1946 Foreigners Act Central Government alone could authorise the extradition of a foreigner, and that the matter in the words of Central Government was still 'Pending further decision'. As this was the position I asked that the case against the doctor should be dropped. In an icy silence I was served tea, and told that he could not help me.

Before seeing the Commissioner of Police I had seen Security Control. There, in an office piled ceiling-high with papers and files, I talked to the Investigating Officer, the IO as he was known. He launched into a tirade against the doctor about how he had demonstrated in Calcutta over the illegal export of children from Bangladesh and how he might do the same thing if there was something he did not approve of in India. He went on and on. . . I felt I had achieved nothing, only the growing conviction that West Bengal simply wanted Jack out.

Once again it was back to the court, to be told the magistrate was sick, and that the case was delayed for another day.

I rang the BHC and told them the whole thing was taking too long, and sent a telegram to the Member of Parliament in Delhi, who wished to be kept informed, telling him that the doctor was still inside, and asking for his help.

The next development was that the solicitor said we should have the hearing on Tuesday, August 4th. All that day we waited but again the case did not come up. The solicitor said the magistrate was not a sympathetic one, and now we must wait for Wednesday, but that everything would be all right; the doctor would be granted bail; it would all be settled.

On the Wednesday I went to the British High Commission early to ask them to be present in the court at one p.m. as this was the time set for the hearing; they agreed to be there.

The day was hot as we sat for a while in the chicken coop outside Alipore Court, discussing the last-minute legal arrangements. Bhattarcharjee's senior partner was to make the 'Prayer to the Magistrate'. The representative from the BHC arrived and we went into the hot, stuffy courtroom. Case after case was called, taking on average about three minutes each.

Then Dr Preger's was called. At last it was all happening. Bhattarcharjee's senior partner made an impassioned plea to the magistrate. He spoke of a renowned doctor, a specialist in TB, indicating his work to the service of the poor. The noisy court became quieter, his voice grew stronger. (Jack was neither renowned, nor a specialist, but the oratory was splendid).

The Indian Red Cross certified that they needed the services of such a doctor. Some of the solicitors rose to their feet; they beckoned me forward; everyone was listening. The prayer concluded 'That the petitioner prays for bail and there is no chance of him absconding or evading trial, if he is enlarged on bail for the sake of the poor community, those who are deprived of proper treatment.'

"Bail granted." It was all over.

It had taken not three, but twenty minutes, and the court was still humming as we left. The BHC's representative was evidently pleased. "Call and see us," he said. The solicitor said that the release papers would now have to go up to the prison to be signed. I took them back to Alipore Special Jail and saw Jailor Gupta. He said the release would take place the next day, the formalities would need to be completed first, and that I could come in the morning at 11.30 a.m.

In the event, by the time the last papers were signed, it was after three in the afternoon when the release finally took place. Unshaven since he was arrested, and carrying a plastic bag with a few things in it, Jack left the prison. The guards and prisoners smiled their farewells, many sorry to lose him. He would return, he told them, with the things the other prisoners needed, but their concern went deeper than that. It was him they needed, not things.

Having broken a tooth on prison bread Jack, after his release, had to have the root extracted. Amoebic dysentery started four days after he got out of prison and reduced him to a wreck within the next fortnight. He was too weak to travel to Delhi to get confirmation from Central Government that he had their permission to work in India, as they had promised him in July, 1981.

Two days before the next hearing was due to take place Jack and I discussed the question of corruption in Indian Prisons. I had not mentioned the money that I had paid to the solicitor, allegedly for the Public Prosecutor, as it was something that I had decided to do, because I felt it was so important for the poor and destitute to have the doctor back, and also because I feared he would become sick if he stayed in the jail, which did in fact happen. I had never had a suitable moment to discuss it with him in the prison; also I thought he might advise against paying it. So it was my decision and my responsibility. But I realised that this was the moment I could no longer keep it to myself and had to tell Jack. So I said that I knew the system was corrupt, and could prove it. I had sold my camera to get the 500 rupees demanded by Mr Bhattarcharjee, who had been recommended by Mr Gupta of Alipore Special Jail.

Since coming out of the prison, Jack had returned there to take in supplies for the prisoners and to visit one of them. He had also written to the Inspector General of Prisons, Government of West Bengal, asking for certain reforms on the grounds of humanity.

Barely two weeks after his release Dr Preger again presented himself at the court as ordered; we saw the solicitor at one o'clock and he asked us to wait outside the court for the case to be called. He appeared a little distant, and I wondered why because usually he was noticeably friendly. After half an hour before the case was called, a man came up to Jack with a great sheaf of papers which he asked Jack to take. Jack said "Give them to my solicitor," and asked him who he was. The man did not reply, but left. We presumed he was from Security Control.

When the case was called and we went into the court Bhattarcharjee, the solicitor, was absent. The magistrate passed the same sheaf of papers over the top of the high desk.

"Sign them," he barked.

"I have no solicitor," Jack answered.

"Don't sign them," I said.

"Get another solicitor," said the Magistrate.

Jack was left standing with the papers in his hand. The whole thing was a 'fix'. They said one of the bondsmen had withdrawn [and clearly the solicitor had too] and that the doctor was to be taken back into custody. Jack once more gave me his keys, his watch, and this time there was an umbrella as well. Carrying all these I left the court, once more in search of a solicitor.

"Be quick," they called, "the time is almost up."

This time I went to the Bar Association where I saw a man I took to be a lawyer.

"I urgently need a straight solicitor," I said.

"I am a solicitor," the man replied.

"Then please will you help Dr Preger, whose solicitor has deserted him," I said. "He is about to be taken into custody, and has just lost his bondsman because the previous solicitor has not paid him, although he has received about 750 rupees from me, but has never submitted an account or given a receipt!"

The Bar Association building, where I found the new man, is in the centre of the complex so we had little time to lose as we hurried back to the court, stopping to buy a special bond sheet, and a stamp. We got through the dwindling crowd at the door.

"I've got a lawyer," I called to Jack, and then, pushing through the last of the crowd, I introduced them. By this time the new lawyer had spoken to the magistrate, and the fix — because that is what it was — had begun to fizzle out. But it was by no means over; there were only about fifteen minutes in which to find another bondsman.

While this was being attended to we sat in the court going through a list of things that needed to be seen to if Jack had to go back inside. Meanwhile, a second bondsman came up to us, to claim at great length that he too had gone unpaid by our late lawyer, Bhattarcharjee.

Then the new solicitor proved himself to be a winner — he came up with a new bondsman.

While we were waiting, the police had locked the doors of the court. We were both inside, with an armed guard sitting three seats behind us. Throughout, the police had not allowed Jack to move from where they had made him sit.

After all the excitement, the leaving was quite quick and once again the doctor was free. The solicitor came back to the International Guest House with us. Sitting on the steps, with a surprised expression on his face, was the plain clothes policeman from Security Control who was our constant shadow.

"Good evening," we said, and turning to the solicitor, "This is our own Security Control!" we explained.

Alipore Special Jail

CHAPTER VII

KALA PRADHAN

Calcutta's Elephant Man

Amrita Bazaar Patrika

CHAPTER VII

Kala Pradhan

A LTHOUGH we knew that Jack's case was likely to go
on from hearing to hearing, he was out of prison, and
being on bail gave him a certain degree of safety in that he was
to some extent protected by the law.

It was a very busy time, with the work to organise each day in
order to use Jack's helpers to the best advantage. On a typical
day we set out with a list of medicines to be bought (those of
which the doctor did not have a supply) as well as bandages,
dressings, cotton wool, gentian violet crystals, and so on. There
was the powdered milk to be made up into individual rations
from the large economical cans and vitamin tablets to be
counted for the TB patients. There were accounts to be kept
and medicines to be distributed to waiting patients. With each
prescription was the name of the patient and a description of
exactly where and in which part of the flyover he lived. As we
have already seen, the flyover was divided into Flyover North,
Flyover South and so on. 'Under Howrah Bridge', 'The Ghat'
or 'Jaganath Ghat' were other areas, and finally the most
particular location had to be described: by which lamp post or
opposite which house number, if it was on a street. Some were
quite bizarre. Lionel Shaw, for example, who was a TB patient,
lived among the dead at the abandoned British Cemetery. Sick,
he lived out his days among the ornate tombs whose cherubic
angels cast robust shadows at midday. But Lionel Shaw will not
join the English dead, for he belongs to the living in Calcutta:
the doctor has got a place for him in a sanatorium.

Getting the prescriptions out could take over an hour. The
destitute cannot be given money to buy medicines for

85

themselves because they are likely to use it to buy food instead. An uncertain sense of priorities for survival, perhaps. The medicines were always given in small doses, sufficient for three days. This increased the administrative work, especially as the doctor was not permitted to open a dispensary at the flyover, so the helpers always had to seek out the patient for the prescribed medication. (Only the very sick and immobile remained in one place all day). Every new tube of ointment or bottle of antiseptic — in fact every prescription — had the label scored with a pen, or the trade name removed, to ensure that it was not resold. The exceptions were the TB patients who were aware of the importance of their daily medication, and were given a month's supply at a time, together with a few others who came to know and understand.

Then there were those who had to be taken to hospitals as out-patients for X-rays, tests and surgery. Again the taxi was the most useful form of ambulance. Unfortunately the doctor's landrover and another vehicle had been left behind at the time of his deportation from Bangladesh and were still in that country. For really sick people travel by bus is virtually impossible. They cannot stand it, nor do the other passengers care to have destitutes on board.

One of the patients brought to Jack from an outlying village was Mokul Dutta, a young child of five years of age. She had a suspected Fallots Tetralogy, (a serious heart condition), and an operation to save her at the Intensive Cardiac Department, at the Calcutta Medical Research Centre, would have cost the equivalent of over £700. I decided to write to a friend in Rome who knew someone with Burroughs Wellcome in England, to see if it was possible to arrange funds for her. In the end that came to nothing, but Father Edward Booth, a Dominican friend, was about to return to his college in Cambridge and wrote to say he would do what he could to help while he was there. I wish I could have heard the sermon he preached for amazingly, the next day there was a telegram to say that the appeal for the child had raised a third of the sum required, then, later the same day, even more incredibly, another telegram arrived to say that the balance had been made up by an anonymous donor. I could hardly believe it, and have kept the telegrams to this day. The second had said 'acknowledge.' That was easy. I almost ran down Park Street to the Overseas Telegraph Office, which never closes, and cabled thanks from the doctor, myself and the parents, and of course, on behalf of the child, Mokul.

Telling her parents that the operation was now possible was the next thing, but, as the doctor pointed out, there was a chance that the child might not survive it, or that on surgical investigation the case might prove to be inoperable.

When the money came through from Rome, via the Vatican Bank, we were afraid that the Government might block it. I took three separate taxis to reach the bank, and walked miles out of my way so as not to be followed. Since I started work at the flyover I had been followed everywhere in Calcutta by plain-clothes security men, and had begun to take them for granted. This time I took care to avoid them. Once there, I asked if the business could be transacted away from the counter, because a large sum was involved. They showed me upstairs. I asked for stapled notes, so that there would be no mistake in counting the thousands of rupees that made up the sum. Then I packed the bundles of notes into my clothes and walked out of the bank a few pounds heavier! As I left I caught sight of my 'tail,' coming in through the plate glass doors. I jumped into the first taxi that I could see, parked just down the road. It was a relief to know that so far as money went nothing could now stop the operation from taking place.

To-day, after both exploratory surgery and one complete operation, the child is fit and well. She will go on having treatment, in the form of extra medicines and body-building foods until adolescence. The family is now a happy one, and Mokul a different child. I wish that the unknown donors could all see her.

About this time there were twins born prematurely down at the flyover. Jack said that we should try to get the weaker one into Shishu Bhavan (Mother Teresa's Children's Home), where the sisters might be able to save it. So I took the father with me, and had the baby admitted. The other twin stayed with the mother on the pavement, separated from the tramlines by a row of railings, tucked under a makeshift net to keep off the mosquitoes. It was pathetic. After leaving the home the father went back on the tram, which he wanted to do. I told him I would check on the baby's progress, and would tell him how it was going. I also gave him enough money to go to find out for himself, although I knew that it would be spent on food, and that I was the only one who would be going back to the home.

Two days later the baby died. The sisters had done their best, that I knew. I went down to the flyover in the early morning before breakfast, when the family should still be there before going rag-picking later. They were. Sadly I told them, and took the father to Shishu to collect the little body. The father could not bear to take it, so I held the bundle as one can only ever hold a baby. Although it was completely wrapped there was no doubt as to what it was.

We waited at the kerbside for a taxi. I stopped one. The driver looked at the bundle, shook his head in refusal and drove on. Another did the same This was repeated until the fourth taxi stopped. He went straight to the point. "I will take you if you can give me a certificate from Mother Teresa to prove that the baby died there." He nodded towards Shishu Bhavan.

"Wait," I said, and motioned the father to get into the cab. Carrying the baby's body, I turned back to the children's home and went upstairs amongst the chatter and activities. There by one of the cots was the Sister-in-Charge, so I explained our predicament, and asked her to write out a certificate of death for the child. She did. I went down the stairs through the sturdy plain metal gates where the poor were already gathering for a distribution of milk and medicines, and out to the taxi. I gave the driver the paper, and got into the back. I put my hand on the father's and we went back along the noisy and lively road, teeming with cars, lorries, people everywhere. On my lap lay the little bundle, still and silent — the wages of poverty, malnutrition, and deprivation of decent conditions. I returned them both, the living and dead, to the mother, and to the pavement that was home. Silently, as the father took the body from me at last, the neighbours and friends closed around to comfort him. He stood there, a silhouette in the blue smoke and fumes that crept through the railings, as I went slowly away, for there was nothing that I could say.

THE fevered boy lay against the wall that was crumbling above his head. There were slogans painted on it, and old posters of the goddess Kali. At his temple stood a terracotta pot in which flies had been gathering for hours. He could not wave them away; he had malaria. The boy was about thirteen years of age, though he was not exactly sure. He was a refugee from Bangladesh and his mother was still there; it was she, he had told me some time before, who sent him to India — to Calcutta, only just across the border from the village where he was born. He had not found work and he had joined the street children along Middleton Row — a double amputee boy and two girls. They all lived on the street.

The flies were feasting on the skinny bits of fish in the bowl. They were as brilliant as the blue of a buffetting sea in a gale off the west coast of Ireland, but he would never see such a far-off shore. If he saw that of his own country, he would see more than most of the people who shared his fate.

The story was that he had escaped from a begging syndicate; even in his present state he could be seen feeling for his legs under last year's blanket. Ali, his friend, had lost both legs to a syndicate. Another girl had lost her lower right arm. There was a four-year difference, but the healing of the wounds of both children appeared somewhat similar, suggesting the same butcher.

The boy was restless. What fears were being magnified in his mind by the burning fever? He had turned over to face the wall again. The rat on whose territory he trespassed was peeping from a crack in the masonry. Its eyes were level with the boy's. He had pulled the blanket up to cover his head so that it would not bite him. There was a scrap of cereal under the stone that was his pillow.

Chandra was also looking down on him. She had crossed over from the street pump, which he was too sick to reach, to bring him some water in a coconut shell. She poured it down his throat; all of them could drink like that. Exhausted, he lay back, as I left them both to fetch the doctor.

The sun was low now and Dr Jack, as the children knew him, lifted the boy from the pavement, off the piece of corrugated paper, his mattress. The leaden arms were hooked about his neck. I called the taxi to come as close as possible. For a moment the boy's eyes met mine, and I bent forward and reached under the stone. I put the comb into the hand he held out limply and wrapped the thin blanket over his shoulders. All destitutes keep their most precious things under their pillows.

We took him to Pren Daan, one of Mother Teresa's homes for sick men, women and children. Gradually he recovered. The sisters looked after and cared for him; he had not had the dreaded cerebral malaria, and after some days he was well enough to leave. He returned one early morning soon after dawn to Middleton Row, to his friends, the street children, and to his pavement. Under his arm was the blanket, and in his hand the comb.

EVERY Saturday morning Kala Pradhan was waiting by nine o'clock outside the Y. He was Calcutta's 'Elephant Man,' a forty-five year old victim of von Reclinhausen's Disease of the Nerves, Neurofibromatosis. Kala is by the nature of his disease very noticeable, for he is disfigured and was then becoming increasingly deformed. Looking at him and talking to him, one was aware that he was a most gentle person. His right eye was untouched by the ravages of the disease, but inside the exterior of that twisted and distorted face his left eye and, on the same side, his lower cheek and mouth, were already being deformed by the tumours which, since the first indications of the disease when he was ten years old, had progressed unrelentingly. The disease is heriditary, and reconstructive surgery is the only treatment available.

Neurofibromatosis is mercifully rare. In England in the early 1900s there was an 'elephant man' who was the subject of a film of the same name in which John Hurt, in the title role, won many awards.

When the ten year-old Kala first became ill he was in his home village in the Balasore district of Orissa. His family had no money, and, like thousands of other villagers, no land. There was no future in Balasore. He was uneducated like many others in the same area. The village already realised that he was different, and so he followed the course adopted by many other teenagers, although from more intense and agitated emotions. He left Orissa by train to become a beggar in Calcutta. He has never been back.

Jack had been giving him a small allowance over the years, and he had a shelter in the Bhowanipore district of Calcutta. It was from his 'home' there (a balcony) that he walked each Saturday to see Jack, to receive his allowance and be taken to the SSKM Hospital, or the PG, as it is more commonly called, to attend the clinic of the plastic surgeon Mrs Sita Roy Chowdhury. Over the span of six months' visiting, and later during Kala's time in hospital, I came to know Mrs Chowdhury well, and also the Resident Medical Officer, with whom I had an extended, polite, but nevertheless continual battle of wills.

Kala and I had been going to the PG together for six months.

Each Saturday we would set out by taxi, to keep Kala from preying eyes; many thought he was a leper, including Neil O'Brien MLA, who later said he had seen us going off together in the taxi, and was curious about where we were going. This he mentioned when I went to enlist his help as a member of the Legislative Assembly. He had, in turn, helped me by suggesting that I should give the story of 'Calcutta's Elephant Man' to the press in Calcutta. I said I'd do anything to get Kala admitted, for the plastic surgery that Mrs Chowdhury advised would improve the patient's ability to eat, and also help his right eye. Nothing, we all knew, could cure or check the disease, but surgery could help Kala in these practical ways. He was consistently patient, sitting waiting each Saturday in the crowded out-patients department of the Plastic Surgery Clinic from 9 a.m. to 12.30 p.m.

After the initial consultation with the surgeon and the RMO, the reason for the visit was to apply for a bed; this had to be done each week. There was no system for advising you when a bed was available. At the same time I always made a point of seeing the RMO on Kala's behalf, while he waited. Sometimes he was examined; always he was stared at by other patients who were also waiting their turn, many of them obviously needing plastic surgery.

We used to get tea from the little tea-boy who over the months became my friend and guide, for there was no corner of the PG that the child did not know, although he was little over ten years of age. He brought the tea in those tiny terracotta bowls, always so hot to hold, which are thrown away after use; the grounds of the hospital were strewn with them. There we used to sit, until yet another Saturday passed with no bed for Kala.

He sat, hiding his face with his thin shawl, concealing the more deformed part of it from the probing eyes and relentless stares of other people. As he was evidently with me, this added to the general curiosity. Bearing all this in mind, and its effect on Kala Pradhan, I felt that he had had enough, so when the opportunity came to invite the press to take up his story I was frankly delighted. I was convinced that we would at last get him a bed.

An interview was arranged at the offices of the Oxford University Press, of which Neil O'Brien was a director. It had gone quite well with the journalist from *Amrita Bazar Patrika*, Mr

Nag, and we had discussed every point. It was arranged that the reporter would come with Kala and myself on the first Saturday that suited him.

Abhijit Nag and Kala arrived at the same time and I introduced them outside the Y, having warned Kala previously that the press were going to help. The doctor had also explained it to him, and Kala had accepted it, and was in favour of the plan. So he was happy enough, that particular Saturday, as we got into the taxi together to cover the seven minute journey to the PG.

That morning at the PG I was reminded of the many other hours that I had spent there during the past year. It was now eight months since I had first been to the hospital. I had accompanied TB patients for Mother Teresa, and a young girl, Chanandra, who had a hole in her heart. She was one of the children of a family who lived on the roof, and worked at Mother Teresa's Kalighat. She had been operated on successfully here. I remembered her and countless others who had come and gone, including several accident cases. But today when the journalist came with us to the hospital, I was thinking chiefly of the job in hand, to get Kala in.

Leaving Kala on the bench, I took the reporter through to the hall outside the office. It was thronged with people pushing and pressing around the door and desk. It was the usual free-for-all. Mrs Chowdhury saw us and I indicated that I wanted to introduce her to my companion. She left the desk and came over to us. We followed her out into a little room off the hall and I told her that I had brought Mr Nag from *Amrita Bazar*, who was interested in the case of Kala Pradhan, and wanted to know what the plans were for his operation. I was afraid at this point that he was going to abscond. He found my direct approach gave him little room to manoeuvre. That was intentional. I did not want a story about 'Elephant Men' and a history of the disease, and when he talked to the consultant I had fears that that was all we were going to get. I therefore thought it wise to say to him, in an audible aside, that we wanted Kala Predhan admitted for the operation that the consultant, Mrs Chowdhury, had advised for the last six months. I was aware that they were fellow countrymen, and that Mr Nag was now engaging in relaxed conversation with her, so I said at the first pause in their conversation that both Neil O'Brien and I felt sure that Mrs Chowdhury would be operating on Kala shortly, and asked if she could settle the question of the bed, now, while the journalist from *Amrita Bazar* was here? Steam-rollered into having at least to make a decision, she suddenly turned and almost ran from the room, out of the hall, and into the RMO's Office, and from there up the stairs to the wards, her sari floating out behind her. The journalist looked a little pale, but I told him he had done wonders, and that we would have a bed for Kala in half an hour. We did. Mrs Chowdhury returned to say that he could be admitted immediately. The goal had been achieved.

The journalist smiled and I thanked him. We went to tell Kala who had been waiting in his quiet way on one of the benches. He was delighted that his waiting was over. There were the formalities to attend to, and there would be things that he would need. I promised to come back with those. I was asked to go to the RMO's Office, but not before more photographs of Kala had been taken for *Amrita Bazar*. Eventually I asked the photographer to stop, as people were watching and I felt it was embarassing for Kala. Very soon he and I were able to go up to find his bed.

Mrs Chowdhury, who had calmed down since Kala's admission, now told me that she would be going away shortly, and did not propose operating until after her return in mid January. Meanwhile Kala was quite safe 'decorating' the ward until we both got back. It happened that I had to go to England for three weeks, and this was obviously the best time to go.

IN England, in January, 1982, the country was in the grip of a hard winter. I was snowed out of Gloucestershire, and almost snowed up in London, where I was staying, seeing to the many things related to Dr Preger's work that needed to be done while I was there. I took advantage of the weather to go to Whitechapel, to The London Hospital, for the 'London', as it is called, holds the medical history of Merrick, the London elephant man, including, in the teaching section of the Hospital Museum, his skeleton. The skull was pathetically similar in shape to Kala's own head, the lengthened chin especially. John Merrick, who had been given living quarters there, was helped by Sir Frederick Travers, a professor at the Royal College of Surgeons. After being exhibited as a freak elephant man by a showman, Merrick had run away, and was fortunate enough to be befriended by Travers.

93

Christopher Kennard, PhD., MRCP, the consultant neurologist at the London Hospital, was of the opinion that Kala was going to receive the correct sort of surgery to open his mouth and let him eat more satisfactorily, and did not feel that any more could be done for him in England than could be done in India. Those of the consultant's colleagues who were more fully conversant with the history of the elephant man were facinated to see the photographs that Jack had taken of him in Calcutta. I was glad to have this second opinion from them, for at the back of my mind was the thought that if they felt there were other possibilities open, then somehow we might have to get Kala to London.

The three weeks in England had been well spent; I had seen a lot of people and been brought up to date with events. But now, after the bitter cold and the snowed-up Gloucestershire countryside, it was lovely to be back in the sun. Delhi, however, was not very hot and I had to have an electric fire on and buy an all-wool shawl in the air-conditioned underground market.

I wondered how Kala was getting on. He was at least tucked up and warm in hospital, even if he was bored with waiting for his operation. I hoped that being in a ward with so many sick would not make him too apprehensive, but it would have been impossible not to have taken up the bed. He would never have got it again and Mrs. Chowdhury was due back soon.

IN January, 1982, because I had been advised I might not be allowed to re-enter Calcutta, I travelled back via Afghanistan and Kabul. With Afghan Airlines the luggage allowance was smaller than that permitted on Indian Airlines, and at London's Heathrow there was a frenzy of unpacking, and reorganising of belongings; in the end I managed with three BEA shoulder bags, and my typewriter. A friend who was with me went home laden with my excess things; if she had not been there it would have been most difficult.

The flight, Moscow-Kabul-Delhi, proved a colourful one. That evening we flew into Moscow, where enormous snow-ploughs were spuming up snow like whales in a calm sea. There were high birch trees in the distance illuminated by floodlights, their pretty barks highlighted by the brightness of the beams. I expected to see a troika at any moment, but only the customary gangway steps were pushed up to the aeroplane, a party of Russian gentlemen boarded, and the flight was resumed. It was not long before it was clear that most of them had been drinking heavily, and even more clear that they intended to carry on doing so.

The vodka bottles came out of pockets and brief cases, persian-lamb headgear was abandoned, and the female staff could not control one of them who wished to leave by the nearby emergency exit; more help was called for from fore-cockpit control, and a male steward took his place at the passenger's side until we reached Kabul in the morning.

I WAS fascinated to be flying into Kabul, where I would change to an Afghan Airlines DC10. The mountains and everything below were a dun colour, a dull brown. As we came slowly down, there, on either side of the runway were rows of camouflaged tanks and helicopters, with Russian red star markings, all their long guns pointing at the runway. The tanks were rugged up against the bitter Afghan winter, and so too were the helicopters. The straight row seemed endless against that dun-coloured ground. We came to a halt between them. The runway was set within an encircling backcloth of the mountains through which we had flown. The gangway was wheeled up, we were told to disembark and proceed to the airport for formalities. The building could be seen at this point. It was small and well-guarded.

As we went down the gangway we were shepherded into a straggling crocodile with the help of Russian guards, rifles slung over their shoulders and an Alsatian dog apiece, held on a strong chain lead. The guards were well dressed against the weather, which in fact felt warmer than it had been in London; they were wearing heavy greatcoats, thick boots, trousers and caps. There were two guards to each person, one on either side of us. There was no question of doing a bit of sightseeing!

They escorted us to the building where we went through the usual formalities. There was a counter at one end, with some assorted handicrafts for sale. But I had no available money at this stage, and anyway I was too interested in the general atmosphere to concentrate on them. We were kept together, in a group. Very shortly another plane taxied round to the runway outside the waiting room.

Once more we were moved out across the tarmac to the waiting plane that was to carry us over the famous North West Frontier to Delhi. I hoped that I could have a window seat, so

95

that I could at least look down on the terrain that had always intrigued me, and which until now had only been known to me on celluloid, peopled by handsome film stars on galloping chargers. The Afghans that were at the airport were certainly equally fine-looking.

Subsequently, in December 1984, I was interested to read in an article in *The Times*: 'In September the Afghan Airlines' only DC10 was badly damaged by a rocket as it landed.'

The aircraft took off, the tanks with their long guns slipped from sight, we climbed up and up, and excitement took hold of me; I had been given a window seat and I was almost back in India.

DELHI was busy and I got a taxi to the New Delhi Y. From there I telephoned journalist friends and made appointments. The next hearing date for Jack Preger's case against being deported was February 4th, and I wanted to get back to Calcutta for it. At that moment the most important thing for me was that at 3.30 p.m. local time I had checked into Delhi; I was safely back in India. It was a wonderful feeling.

INTERLUDE

Rajdhani Express

INTERLUDE

BEHIND the impressive façade of the Secretariat in New Delhi — designed by Herbert Baker in conjunction with Lutyens — were the Indian corridors of power of Central Government, eight miles of them. The last time I had seen parts of the Secretariat was six months earlier, when the doctor was waiting for the advice and opinion of the Minister of Home Affairs over the question of his latest 'Quit India' notice. I remembered wryly the words of Queen Victoria that I had seen at the time, painted in a semi circle around an archway leading off from a large domed hall in a part of the secretariat across the road. These stated, in large clear gold-edged letters, three sentences, the last being 'in their gratitude our best reward.' Now, I was here again, this time to seek help from the highest authority — Prime Minister Indhira Gandhi. I was going to Gate 6, South Block, the gate for the Prime Minister's Office.

It was cool enough to be wearing a fine wool shawl, Indianwise, over that most English of garments, the 'puffa.' The wind was blowing at it slightly as I crossed the wide road between the great blocks of the Secretariat complex where it runs down as straight as a die to the triumphal arch, India Gate, a landmark set in the middle distance. Once across, and on the other side of the road, I walked along the outside of the buildings in their deep shadows until, across a large forecourt, I reached Gate 6 of South Block, and passed in through the ample doorway. Inside there was a large polished desk covered with telephones at the right hand side of the reception hall, beyond which there was an imposing staircase. At the bottom were groups of men talking in twos and threes, well and suitably dressed. The general atmosphere was of quiet businesslike efficiency. I explained to the dark-suited official who had come forward that I had not been aware of it early enough to take

99

advantage of the *darshan*, the early morning reception that Mrs Gandhi held at her residence in Safdajang Road between 8 a.m. and 10 a.m. each day, and that if it was possible to give her a letter or even to see her, it would be a great help to me.

The sympathetic official said I could go up to Mrs Gandhi's office where I could talk about it to her personal assistant and see what could be arranged.

Everything was quietly impressive and sombre in decoration, the corridors powerful in their silence. I passed no one on my way to the office of the personal assistants to the Prime Minister.

The room, when I reached it, was formal. There were about three assistants working, each concentrating on the papers before him. One of them listened while I explained the bare bones of the situation. He said he would try to get an appointment with Mrs Gandhi for me that day. Meanwhile he suggested I write a letter, then and there, which could be given to her directly. He passed me some writing paper and I sat, the blank sheet before me, at the large table which seemed to fill half the room. With the whole complicated situation running through my mind, I decided that the only letter I could write without setting out the case in detail, which I could not do without all the documentation, would be to write, as they say, from the heart. Apart from giving the particulars of the case, i.e. that Dr Jack Preger, MA (Oxon), a British National and medical practitioner, again faced trial in West Bangal for allegedly contravening the Foreigners Act, Section 14, I appealed to her as Prime Minister to intervene personally on his behalf, and placed confidence in that hope. It was in the circumstances the best I could do.

The personal assistant read it. "It is important," he said, and added that he would take the letter straight in to Mrs Gandhi. If it was possible to arrange a meeting he would contact me. He knew that my place on the overnight express to Calcutta was booked. I thanked him and left the room, going out once more into the heavily-carpeted corridor, past a figure waiting on one of the elegant seats, strategically placed by another heavy door: a Punjabi, wearing a fine turban, a reminder that this was India, and not the Athenaeum. I was impressed. No one had refused me entry, or even asked to take, or keep, the black plastic bag that I carried with the relevant papers in it and the two security men had been helpful.

The day was warm, and the sky pale blue. An impeccably-mounted standard bearer stood outside the iron gates, a slight impatience betrayed by a gentle lifting of his steed's hoof. Like me, he too was waiting. . .

New Delhi. January 20th, 1982
AS the Rajdhani Express rattled its way across India, with Hindi music characteristically playing over loud speakers, the story of Dr Preger continued, and perhaps its end or even its beginning; for at his trial on the 4th February he faced deportation or imprisonment. However, the 'Lonely Crusader,' as the *Business Standard* called him, was no longer alone — behind him was the press of India, backed by the British press and television services.

India's Elephant

CHAPTER VIII

The Living Destitute

CHAPTER VIII

The Living Destitute, January 1982

I N Calcutta, I came through the narrow corridor from the broad winding staircase at the PG Hospital, through the passageway packed with metal beds, and the patients with the remains of their last rice meal on tin plates on the floor beside them. The beds were placed Scutari-like, head to tail, while the nurses in stiffly-pleated saris with crimson epaulets sat over huge ledgers in dusty duty rooms. As I entered the ward I could see Kala sitting up in his cot, that so familiar figure. He saw me, and got up, smiling as he came towards me. It was a long ward and there were patients everywhere. The atmosphere was of pain and distress, but some people smiled. We met. I touched him, took his arm, and as I looked at him I saw that from his good eye tears crept down his cheek.

"Show me round," I said. We walked along and out on to the balcony, and past the patients whom evidently he now knew, and I thanked Heaven that I had got back to India.

KALA was operated on at the end of January. In March an article appeared in *Amrita Bazar Patrika*, entitled 'Calcutta's Own Elephant Man.' By then Kala was better. His operation, skillfully performed by Mrs Chowdhury, had helped him. He no longer hid one half of his face with the thin shawl and he could eat more easily. We had all visited him during the long and painful weeks. When he was well enough Dr Preger came to talk to him in Bengali and raised the question of his convalescence.

Reviewing the case of Kala Pradhan and the question of his convalescence accentuated the need for a home, from which so many would benefit.

105

Jack wrote to Mother Teresa's Missionary Brothers of Charity asking the Brother-in-Charge, Brother Arvind, if he could find a place for Kala Pradhan when he was discharged from hospital. Jack pointed out that Kala had no relatives, was a destitute, and a beggar, and asked if he could be admitted to Nabo Jibon, the Brothers' Home across the river at Howrah. The answer from Brother Arvind read: 'I am sorry not to admit your patient in Nabo Jibon. We cannot keep any permanent patients in our Dying Home. This house belongs to the dying destitute and emergency patients and suffering patients'. It was signed Brother Arvind.M.C.

This letter shows the problems faced by the living destitute in Calcutta. Many have helped Kala, including a charming group of young people in the Philippines known as the 'Sowers,' and he still has Jack's weekly stipend. But now he also begs, for he has returned to his balcony — a living destitute.

FOLLOWING a considerable amount of publicity in the UK, the BBC decided to make a programme about Jack's work, and he was asked to give an interview with Mark Tully. A local camera crew were hired to film Jack working down at the flyover. This was to be done in the early morning so that the film could be flown back to London to be shown with the interview. The Indian crew were terrified that their equipment would be smashed by the flyover people, so they were in a great hurry to finish. London had particularly said they wanted pictures of the pigs that lived among the people in the shacks along the railway lines. That presented no problem, but conducting the Indian crew around was time-consuming and although we had met them at the station in the early morning and had brought them to the flyover, for the doctor's workers this was just another busy day with a lot of other work to do.

Derek, the Anglo-Indian, was supposed to be taking a woman patient, a suspected TB case, to the PG Hospital for sputum tests, but he was confused by the presence of the camera crew. Meanwhile, there was a new man who was extremely sick with chicken pox and dysentery, so Jack asked me to clean out his mouth and give him as much liquid as he could drink, and then he was to be taken to the Hospital for Infectious Diseases. In the end Derek undertook to take this man and I took his patient to the PG hospital for her tests.

So we all went our separate ways, arranging to meet again at

106

the Oberroi Grand for Jack's interview, which was scheduled for one o'clock. It was to cover Jack's work and also the prospects he faced of deportation or imprisonment that might result from the next hearing. Mark Tully arrived late and executed a nimble-footed 'pas de deux' through the elegant reception hall with Jack, briefing him as we crossed the cool courtyard of that most comfortable hotel, to which we went only when invited by the press. An interview had been set up in the garden, by the swimming pool. It looked more like a setting for *The Great Gatsby* than for conversations on the prospects of prisons and possible deportation. This BBC interview seems to have been a success, judging from the ensuing fan mail, which has never really stopped since.

When the interview was over, Jack and I walked back to Middleton Row. It had been quite a strain. It was interesting to think through all the things that had been covered in it. Back at the Y, Derek reported to Jack on the hospital case. He told us he had had great difficulties as the chicken pox patient had been refused admission at the Hospital for Infectious Diseases, and, after trying others without success, he was now back on the bit of platform he had come from, at Jaganath. This was a blow. The man was very sick. As there were still prescriptions to be done, and other work to be prepared for Derek for the next day, I suggested that I get the patient over to Mother Teresa's Missionary Brothers of Charity over Howrah Bridge, or take him to Sister Luke at Kalighat. But it was late by then, and the sisters left Kalighat at 6.30 p.m., so we had to try the Brothers.

I set out for Howrah, just catching a mini bus at the top of the road for a journey that takes about half an hour. It was rush hour, and dusk. By the time I reached the flyover it was quite dark, and inky under Howrah Bridge. There were people about on the disused platform, the evening fires were starting; some of the people who saw me waved a greeting. One or two came towards me out of the gloom, but I signed then away explaining "I'm going on, I cannot stop."

The darkness stretched out ahead, shrouding the cobbled road. The raised platform was shoulder high on my right. It was quite black but then, suddenly, there was a light. I felt it was a beacon burning for me, as by my reckoning it was about where the patient should be. I walked steadily on, thinking about how I could get the man across the bridge and whether there would be a rickshaw, and then I came to the light. It was a

107

solitary piece of candle stuck on to the cobbles. Beside it, a joss stick was smoking, stuck into an orange, at the head of the man I had come to find. He was dead.

The people crowded round me. I told them to leave everything as it was, including the candle, and that I would report his death to the police (so that there would be no trouble). I said I would explain that he was sick, and I would bring them back with me.

I left them and walked back to the *thana* (police station) at the flyover. One of the men walked with me to the main road. I went into the *thana*. It was not the first time I had been there on a similar errand. There had been another body before, last summer, on the ghat, which someone had called me over to see. That one I had signed in too, just as I was to do now. 'The left-handed memsahib,' the police had called me, they remembered.

WHEN I had explained why I was there a great hefty policeman took his torch, and said that he would come with me to see the body. "But," he remarked, "it is dangerous down there; bad people."

Clearly he was reluctant to go. The police make raids against the people there from time to time.

The destitute were all too familiar with trouble from the police. Later Dr Preger reported, for instance, that 'In mid-July 1983 Calcutta police destroyed a squatters' settlement on the railway line at Jaganath Ghat, adjacent to Howrah Bridge, which crosses the Hoogly River. The railway line is to be used as part of the proposed Circular Railway. At present the line serves the docks and is hardly used. No alternative accommodation was provided and the squatters alleged that the police burnt some of their huts — which the police denied. More than a hundred huts were pulled down. Also a school, and all the families left homeless (in the middle of the monsoon). Many of the families remain sheltering on an adjacent loading platform, from which they were previously dislodged.'

I said to the policeman he need not worry, that they knew me, and would never hurt me, and that he could walk behind and shine the torch, which he did.

When finally I got back Jack said "You were too quick; did something go wrong?"

108

"Yes," I answered, "we did not get to the Brothers; he was already dead."

The man had been a Moslem and had only arrived that morning at the flyover, so no one had known him. I was glad that they had lighted the candle for him, and I often think of that night, remembering the darkness and that solitary light. These are the times when I want to go back most; when I shall be glad that this book is finished, written for those flyover people who ask for so little and should be given so much.

Living by the railway lines

CHAPTER IX

MIDDLETON ROW AND THE SEVENTEENTH COURT HEARING

To think my most enemies my best friends

Sir Thomas More

CHAPTER IX

December 1982 — Middleton Row and the 17th Court Hearing

THE armed guards outside the State Bank of India guard, for the most part, the relentless generator that shakes its way through the heat of the day, never stopping to consider its effect on the ears of those engaged on columns of figures in the vibrating, dusty offices within the building. On the street outside, a child destitute bursts a balloon with a shot-like explosion that draws a covert glance from the Security Control policeman, who is usually keeping watch outside the Y. He squats reading a Hindi newspaper, his back to the wall of the International Guest House, (the Y), while he studies the white ankles of the foreigners walking past. Often they are those of volunteers working for Mother Teresa at one of her homes or houses; Shishu Bhavan, the Children's Home perhaps, or Pren Daan, or Kalighat; perhaps they are just shopping for a Campa orange at the tiny stall where the owner sits Buddha-like, in a continual Lotus position, in a square recess set into the wall of the building which is his street stall. This is raised about four feet from the ground level so that, seated, he looks down on his customers from behind the coke and Campa orange bottles and the empties, dispensing coke, lifebuoy soap, and candles while filling green leaves with the betel nut that he keeps in an open-necked brass container in front of him.

On one side of the Row are blocks of apartments. A sturdy great palm tree reaches three quarters of the way up the raw sienna walls of the green-shuttered flats and another rather pretty whispy tree grows beside it. A baboon hides in it, after running like an old man along the ledge from the bank, ducking its head as it races under a succession of open windows. It then leans drunkenly over to see the effect of its marathon on the open-mouthed children below, whose white tongues foam with ice-cream from the vendor's barrow. They stop playing street cricket and look up to see not the hard wooden ball, but the softness of a black muzzle, and two beady eyes, in a halo of grey hair.

On the opposite side is the International Guest House or Galway House, the names representing different eras in its history. It is known affectionately as the Y, loved perhaps not only for its shortcomings, but also because it is home for all who rest — or try to — in its shade. They are absorbed into its life, protected by its formidable secretary, of mixed oriental ancestry, whose enchanting, doll-like grandchildren demonstrate this to advantage. She governs all with a calmness Buddha would have extolled.

The story goes that during a fire in a previous managerial position, she had the presence of mind to count the linen down which escapees slithered to safety! The boys, the sweepers and the bearers continue over the years to serve, and the same dhobi sits waiting for the laundry at the foot of the broad staircase, every day before, during and after breakfast.

Almost next door is the Xerox duplicating office, where I can get photocopies done, if the originals are sharp and clear. If pale and delicate they have to be taken round to the Russell Street Xerox shop, where the machine is superior and the cost of copies higher; but on this occasion it is the office next door that is doing the copying for me, so I am waiting with my coffee before me in the little café-cum-restaurant known as My Fair Lady. It has the original figure of a transformed and elegant Eliza Doolittle, painted in white on the glass door that I have rarely seen shut. The espresso machine, whether working or not, is polished as brightly as the sceptre of England. Jacobean raised flower designs swirl in ultramarine plastic over the seats of metal fold-up chairs, and a golden amber-winged cockroach crosses the red stained floor, avoiding a curved section of an eggshell as it reaches the cliff-like erosion of the blue and cream wall. In response to the flip-flopped foot of the waiter it turns two somersaults before changing direction, in a strategy designed to confuse those engaged in avoidance tactics.

The best local telephone rests on a rough shelf; calls cost one rupee each. Beside the photo trails a convincing but undusted imitation plant; higher, and poised to fly — like a Phoenix from

114

the ashes — is a china duck, blue flash-markings on its clumsy wings. Across the small room an orange marigold-head garland hangs above the photograph of the Director of the Water Works of Calcutta, who was the original owner of the café. A small dirty cup holds a bunch of immaculate straws, and the music of the Red Baron breaks all meggatone limits in a crescendo of sound that Schweitzer could not have surpassed on his organ, while Bengalis pour in through the open door for chicken tika rolls.

Across the road, the ironing boy sleeps on his barrow, tucked away in an almost invisible crease between the indian-red buildings, which soak up the siesta-time sun. There in his retreat off the street he dreams of better things, while his little unstoked fire is dead by three in the afternoon, enforcing a respite for the black smoothing irons that rest precariously on the rounded coals in the brazier, allowing them to cool gently through the Advent night, till the next dawn.

ON December 7th, 1982, I woke early to the banging of doors, as Mother Teresa's volunteers, who make up a large percentage of the people staying at the Y, were leaving for meditation and Mass at the Mother House of the Missionaries of Charity in Lower Circular Road. It was only 4.30, but there was no point in attempting to sleep again; the crows had already started their strident calling and the day in Calcutta had begun.

It was quite cold under the shower; the water should have been hot but it was not even tepid, for the management had decided to remove the boilers — not during the summer, when it wouldn't have mattered, but in the winter. No doubt when summer came again, the humidity of the city reached ninety-nine per cent and the temperature was something over 110 degrees, the water would again be searingly hot.

Downstairs in the full dining room, breakfast ran its chaotic course; the jam (no marmalade) arrived first, and the coffee last, with eggs, toast and butter fitted in between.

Later, on the verandah, where dark green hangings strung between the archways stopped the progress of wayward tennis balls towards the dusty window panes, I waited for Kala. Suddenly, framed in the front doorway against the sun, I caught sight of his familiar figure. He no longer wrapped the thin and worn shawl around his face to hide his disfigurement, but wore a discreet patch over his bad eye. He greeted me, his

115

hands together in the *Namaste* position, palms and fingers touching, his smile as gentle as ever; to keep him away from the searching eyes of the street beggars, we carefully led him inside the hostel, which he would never have dared to enter on his own. I gave him two bars of soap and the coconut oil that I had bought for him the previous day — it was the usual small parcel wrapped in newspaper and tied with thin string. There was money for him, too, from the youth group in Singapore. The doctor had told him it was there and would be given to him over the weeks ahead. He was still attending the hospital every Saturday to have some additional treatment for the tear duct below his eye.

When he left, Jack and I sat talking for a minute and he told me that a Communist leader, the Marxist Promode Das Gupta had died in Beijing, and that there might be a period of mourning, so once again it was possible that the Court Hearing for which we were waiting would be delayed. The Calcutta *Herald* carried a piece about Gupta saying that he had been given the tribute of a mass attendance at his funeral, and commented that his personal disdain for luxury deserved commendation.

By the middle of the morning we were ready to leave for the court. A cab of the usual vicious yellow was conveniently parked outside the Y, its many layers of thick paint protecting it from the dust and fumes which were already beginning to blow down Middleton Row. We got in and wound up the windows against the fumes, and the taxi drove us off to what was to be Jack Preger's seventeenth court appearance. By this time, although protected by the law, the doctor was a considerable embarrassment to the West Bengal Government who cannot deport him, but will not accept him; in this way they kept dragging things out with one hearing after another.

At an earlier hearing in May, when Jack was seeking permission to visit his sick mother in England and wanted to make sure that he would be allowed back to India, his bail was set at the enormous figure of 500,000 rupees: about £30,000 sterling. The Alipore judge in 1981 had agreed with the Government of West Bengal that the doctor should not be allowed home, because the judge wanted to finish the trial immediately. It was suggested that his family in England should launch a nationwide appeal for this figure, but it would have taken far too long to organise such a task and the matter was urgent. Later that month, after it was put to him that the 500,000 rupees asked was excessive, the judge reduced the figure himself to 20,000 rupees.

In London on May 4th, 1982, the *Daily Telegraph* had published a headline '£30,000 Bond for Briton to see Mother.' It was a column written by Charles Henn, which went on to say 'India has told a British doctor working in Calcutta that he cannot return home to see his seriously ill seventy-year old mother, unless he lodges a £30,000 bail bond with the authorities.' After mentioning the doctor's family in Norfolk, Henn continued 'Paradoxically, he is charged with defying a notice to quit India, served on him last year. If found guilty, he could be jailed for up to five years, or deported.' The article included a photograph of Jack. It went on to affirm what the doctor had repeated both in an interview and when talking generally, that he would go to jail if necessary, because, he said, "then I would be able to work among the prisoners."

On May 8th, the *Daily Telegraph* printed another column, reporting the decrease in the bail figure, and that the authorities in West Bengal had relented, so that the high bail figure had been reduced.

Thanks to the reduction in the bail Jack was then able to make his visit to England.

Now, in December, the taxi hurled its way along the busy streets to Bankshall Street. On that morning many friends in India and in England were thinking of the doctor, while only the week before Dom Bede Griffiths, at Shantivanam, his Ashram in Tamil Nadu, had asked for special prayers both for him and his work. The press, too, had always supported Jack, both in India and the UK. It was good to remember all this.

The taxi stopped abruptly at the red brick Bankshall Court Buildings straggled alongside the road. It was busy there. Through the gates in the large forecourt were milling solicitors, talking, waiting, and hoping for clients. We pushed our way through the entrance. Anything, I thought, anything, could happen here today. A strong sense of unease over the whole legal affair was what had brought me back to India, and to this courthouse in Calcutta after my second visit to England.

The stairway was painted a dark red to shoulder height; it reminded me of the hospital deck on Nelson's flagship *The Victory*. Here, I hoped, it was to disguise the betal nut stains.

Jack had feared the case might not be heard because of

official mourning for Promode Das Gupta, the Marxist chief who had died recently. But the magistrate was sitting as we entered the No. 6 Courtroom.

I looked round the room briefly. It was filthy, with grime and black cobwebs shrouding the dilapidated elegance of a long window that, cleaned and sparkling, could have graced Versailles. Above, the pigeons from their positions on the tops of pillasters near the ceiling, flew to and fro over the Bench, the magistrate, and a group of dusty solicitors huddled behind their long narrow table below the dais and the clerks' table.

The presiding magistrate, his seemingly myopic eyes trailing from one side of the court to the other, did not, I thought, miss much. The room was a semi-circle, a chopped-off section of what had once been a larger one. The floor was made up of heavy, uneven boards, and the rows of chairs were black and rickety. Along one wall were five well-built cupboards with varying padlocks, all locked. Near the dais there was an open one from which, at intervals throughout the day a tea-pot was taken by a bearer who rarely stood upright, but, cringing in deference to the bench, served water from his rose-decorated tea-pot to both the magistrate and the clerk with the reverence of an altar boy.

At 10.45 a.m. there arrived a thin man with a pronounced adam's apple and a long narrow nose, wearing two shades of brown. He was from Security Control. Alongside him came a policeman in customary white ducks, and because it was winter a navy blue uniform sweater; his gun, worn at the belt, snug in its holster, a briefcase in his hands. He sat down next to council for the prosecution, and was to remain sitting there as long as we did; he was witness for the Government of West Bengal, witness to the original arrest of the doctor in his room at the Y seventeen months earlier, in 1981.

Under the Foreigners' Act of 1946 the arrest of a foreigner can only be made by an officer over the rank of Constable.

At eleven the case of Dr Jack Preger was called. Jack rose and moved to a wooden stand with a balustrade decorated with simple carved knobs, but he did not step up into it. Previously, on arrival in the court, he had handed a petition to the Public Prosecutor. This set out formally reasons for asking the court's permission to make a short visit to the restricted area of Darjeeling, for which a permit was required, and was usually issued. The purpose of the visit was a short holiday. At the time

118

there were restrictions because of unrest in the North-east States of India. The section in the Foreigners' Act that deals with the matter of restricted areas reads like the setting for an adventure story, or the beginning of a book on exploration. Section 27 of the Act refers to the definition of a 'Protected Area'. It means any border area falling beyond the inner line of Jammu and Kashmir 'From the point where the National Highway I-A crosses the Punjab/Jammu and Kashmir State boundary along the National Highway up to Jammu — along Ranbir — Canal Road to Akhur — along Chenab River up to the junction of Chenub and Ans River.' The section then continues its way in terms of degrees of latitude and longitude; it takes to mountain passes and follows crest lines over ridges and peaks, and becomes in its descriptions even more picturesque. In this way the Act sets out the inner line in Hamachai Pradesh, Uttar Pradesh, Sikkim, Arunachal, Nagarland, Manipur, Mizoram, as well as Jammu and Kashmir. Jack is particularly attracted to mountains, and under the terms of his bail he is allowed to travel in other parts of India. The Public Prosecutor scanned the document thoroughly and passed it up to the magistrate. At this point the doctor mentioned that the Deputy Commissioner at Security Control, Mr Singh, had no objection to his visiting Darjeeling if the Court agreed. At this stage Jack asked if the case could be delayed because his solicitor Sushansa Datta had failed to appear in Court. This agreed, we all sat down to wait again.

After a while the doctor asked if we might go to look for the solicitor, and see his clerk. The magistrate agreed so we made our way out into the brightness of the mid-morning, passing clusters of solicitors, clients and clerks who are always there talking, or waiting for the cases to be called. At the Bar Members' Association on the far side of the forecourt, we found Datta's clerk sitting on the verandah. Jack asked him where Datta was and pointed out that he should have been present in Court that morning. The clerk was not in the least put out, either by Datta's absence or by our situation, and stayed idling happily on the verandah with his colleagues, enjoying the winter sun.

We took the opportunity to fortify ourselves against the uncertainties of the day with cups of hot sweet tea at the nearest tea-shop, before returning to the greyness of the pigeon-ridden Court No. 6. There was still time for Datta to appear although

119

it now seemed highly unlikely, bearing in mind that he had previously been intimidated by the police at Lalbazaar Police Station when, he claimed, he had been warned not to defend the doctor so skillfully. He was also pressurized at Security Control where, Datta said, he "went in fear of his life."

His was not the only case of intimidation related to the doctor. A committee member of the Indian Red Cross, Mr M. M. Kolay of Jani Road had a similar experience. In his case the police came to his house in the Hoogly District, when Mr Kolay was engaged in collecting signatures for a petition asking the Government of West Bengal to allow the doctor to continue his work. The petition was from the villagers in the Janai Road area. Jack still has this petition. (A copy of the first page shows a list of names with the thumb print of the corresponding person alongside). Mr Kolay told the doctor that he risked being "put in fetters" if he continued to collect signatures for the petition.

Considering these incidents, it was almost certain that Datta was not going to come to court. We had to try to get an adjournment. Another case was now drawing to a close and the solicitors involved were in front of us. Their glistening black hair was worn long, and touched their starched whitesh-grey collars, for nothing is really white in Calcutta. They argued amongst themselves, then the case was abruptly concluded and the stand was again vacant.

It was almost one o'clock. The pigeons swept across the room. No-one bothered to notice them. Pieces of paper passed between lawyers, and another pigeon flew by. Security Control came and went, but the police witness continued to sit bolt upright, waiting his turn. He had no number on his epaulet, only the legend 'Calcutta Police,' but Jack copied down his name from the labelled briefcase that he held firmly in both hands.

The sun shone dimly through the high window, barely penetrating the opaque glass streaked with droppings, and thick with pre-Independence grime.

How could justice be done in such surroundings? What are the long-term answers to all Indian's problems? The spirituality of India is at odds with materialistic development. The ideals of Gandhi and Vinoba Bhave, however worthy as social endeavours, are not, when considered in relation to time and the march of progress, likely to prove an effective counter to

120

Communism; nor will they increase the standard of living of the countless millions living at and below the poverty level in India's cities and urban communities.

The answer will be sought, perhaps in continuing aid from the nuclear societies of the West, or perhaps inevitably in closer relationships with neighbouring totalitarian regimes; but certainly the present massive poverty will not be tolerated indefinitely.

Dr Preger's case was called again, and the proceedings stirred slowly into life. The Public Prosecutor got to his feet and addressed the magistrate. It became clear that the delay caused by the absence of Datta had irritated the PP and that he was set on continuing the proceedings without him. He launched into a tirade against the doctor and his activities in Bangladesh and India, prefacing his attack with a statement in a quiet voice that the doctor's bail bondsmen had surrendered bail, and that the doctor must therefore be taken back into custody.

It was another example of the abandonment that Jack had experienced previously at Alipore Court, when Bhattacha-charjee, the solicitor then acting for him, had given up the case, and the bondsman had given up the surety. Then, as now, the doctor was taken back into custody. During all those hours of waiting, the Prosecution had been aware that the doctor's bail bondsman had surrendered bail, but they had not mentioned the fact. One learns in time that they might pounce late when it is too late to act.

I left the courtroom quickly and retraced our earlier steps towards the Bar Members' Association, threading among the solicitors waiting to be engaged. I glanced about. An unlikely couple were seated on a crumbling low wall. They saw me and stopped their chatter; the younger of the two rose.

"Are you a solicitor?" I asked, to give myself time to examine him as a possible candidate. He was a stooping, tall figure, in the traditional black coat, but worn with flared green trousers. Now, I felt, was not the time to indulge in scruples over the colour of a solicitor's trousers, or the thought that somehow the black and grey striped ones perhaps commanded more respect. I must press on. Thoughts of the courtroom loomed in my mind. I plunged into the now familiar story.

"The solicitor of a doctor being charged under Section 14 of the Foreigners' Act has been intimidated by Security Control and the police, so that he has not appeared in Court to represent

121

his client, who in his absence has been taken back into custody because his bondsman has also surrendered bail. I am asking if you, despite the possibility of intimidation, are prepared to take the case?''

By now both men, for apparently they acted as a pair, were on their feet. ''You have nothing more to fear, we will take care of everything.'' Words I had heard a good many times before.

We struggled back against the people coming out of the building; it was lunch time. On the way into the courthouse, there was a counter where we stopped and bought a petition slip. It would need to be filled in by the solicitors and signed by the doctor. It had a stamp stuck haphazardly across it. Our prayer complete, we entered the courtroom. Inwardly I was concerned at the unlikely appearance of my legal gentlemen, but 'necessity winneth a crown'. If the doctor was surprised he did not show it. When I explained that there were now two solicitors prepared to act for the doctor the proceedings were halted and the solicitors were granted an intermission in which to confer with their client.

Jack outlined to them the basic elements of the case and the present position, and warned them again that, by accepting the case, they might be open to intimidation by the police and Security Control. They assured him that they understood this as I had already told them.

The certificate was signed and I had to go with the younger solicitor to get the 'Prayer to the Magistrate' typed. By now the older solicitor had confided to his doctor client that he had a weak heart and had taken on a younger man to ensure he did not get over tired. The younger one told me that he had a very bad headache, but was prepared to accept one, only one, aspirin for it. Jack meanwhile was suffering from neither of these disabilities, but from another; hunger.

Once again we were outside Bankshall Street Court, this time beyond the busy forecourt and by the railings on the pavement, for here the typists sat working away at their typewriters on improvised desks in front of them. We needed the 'Prayer to the Magistrate' typed up in order to hand it in when the Court reassembled. The prayer must sum up the doctor's situation, the legal position and the question of bail. Huq, for that was his name, the older partner being Bhowmick, dictated to the typist, accompanying his words with a sequence of gestures that would

122

have done credit to the acting profession.

When the prayer was finished Huq started back to the court, while I cast longing looks at piles of bread waiting to be made into toast on a street café's barrow. Toast or the prayer; it was impossible to have both, and I became for that moment a legal agnostic.

Back in the court the magistrate was on the bench and the PO was gently tapping his folder of papers. The police witness sat as still as ever, and the armed guard at the back of the Court continued to shiver, as he surveyed his prisoner; then he smiled at me as he made an exaggerated grimace at the cold. The magistrate accepted the prayer from the solicitors. Meanwhile, the Prosecution demanded that the case be continued. As the papers relating to the doctor's defence were with the ex-solicitor, Datta, there was no question of this; it was a flagrant attempt to use the situation to his advantage. However the magistrate carefully studied the prayer, and then told the Court that he accepted that the doctor was now in the hands of Messrs. Huq and Bhowmick, that a new hearing date would be fixed, and that when that was arranged the doctor could again be released on bail.

That was the end — the magistrate rose. The fingers of the police witness holding the briefcase relaxed. He was not to be called. The Prosecutor left with a glowering look in our direction, and then shortly returned, to exchange some confidence with the clerk of the court. Meanwhile, while bail was being arranged, I ordered tea and toast from the tea-boy who, sensing the need of the moment, had come into the room. We sat quietly waiting, the guard at the back, a few rows behind. The tea was a relief, and the toast a joy.

The bail arrangements were concluded and the doctor was free to go.

Bhowmick, his new solicitor, asked for two rupees for the guard and they were given. "After all," Jack said, "Sir Thomas More tipped his executioner." As we clattered down the stone stairs, the guard still on our heels, he added "Is he coming home with me?"

A Pavement Mother

CHAPTER X

'THE INVISIBLE MILLIONS' OF WEST BENGAL

Man is dependent on inhuman social conditions

Karl Marx

CHAPTER X

The Situation in West Bengal 1983 — 'The Invisible Millions'

A S English aristocrats they are impressive, as soldiers and rulers they were once powerful, as works of art they vary in value, but in reality, sadly, their condition is poor: cracked by the heat and in need of restoration. I refer to the paintings in the portrait section of the Victoria Memorial in Calcutta.

The building, white in the noonday sun, reflects the magnificence of the former Empire, the power of the past Empress, and the stability of another age. All is now passed.

One wanders through the galleries and the whole of the Raj lives again before one: Clive, Curzon, Wellesley, and Mountbatten; names from great days; and then one returns to the streets where over a million people live in dire poverty.

Poverty is excessive, English is still taught in schools but is controversial, trouble menaces the streets, disorder is prevalent. Getting a rail ticket is a battle, boarding the train a greater one. Howrah station is an experience. At the entrance there is a notice in English and Hindi which reads 'We hope you have a happy journey'. Inside the station portals lie the bodies of the destitute who have nowhere to live or die, children, babies; many are refugees from Bangladesh — this is now their only home. To reach the platform or the restaurant you have to pick your way carefully over them; it is pointless to have a suitcase with wheels or a trolley; it would not be possible to move it a couple of inches. The platforms are the same — bodies all the way.

Nehru, writing of Gandhi, spoke of him as a ray of light that pierced the darkness. Gandhi had urged, 'All you who live by their exploitation; get rid of the system that produces this

127

poverty and misery,' while Nehru exhorted 'Get off the backs of the peasants and workers'.

The system that supports this poverty has not been improved by Independence and none of these ideals have come any closer to reality. The destitute lies on his pavement. The sick and dying are wrapped in their poverty, in the stinking open sewers of India, and the lepers beg in every city. Even in Delhi, that seat of Government, they are there now; no politician has removed them from the street.

The grandeur of the British-built Secretariat in New Delhi, now housing the government and bureaucracy of India, has not altered life one jot for the peasant boy, still a child, staggering with an immense load in the early hours of the morning.

Jawaharial Nehru stated that nothing saddened him as much as the sight of children who were denied education, sometimes denied even food and clothing; 'If our children are denied education what is our India tomorrow going to be?' What indeed?

Only negative qualities are found, when one looks at the existing system. The government of West Bengal has a policy, supported and instigated from the highest level, to deter all people who would like to give voluntary help, in medicine, for example, from aiding or helping the absolutely destitute of India. Sometimes it appears that for the Government the important thing is that the caste system should remain intact. Apparently it is a matter of indifference if the poor die. So long as the rich middle-class can eat cream cakes in air-conditioned restaurants, why should they bother? The sick and the dying do not even attempt to beg from them; they already know the answer.

Where the answer should be, there is a vacuum. In order to help the destitute and remove exploitation from the back of the peasant as Gandhi wished, social reform needs to be sought not by the minorities but by the majorities — and this is not likely in the near future in India.

So the row of Empire builders may continue to deteriorate in their ornate gold frames in the Victoria Memorial, and look out unseeingly over the plains of India — their sightless painted eyes echoing the view of those with eyes to see, who, sadly lacking in vision, allow conditions of poverty to exist alongside a rich and sickly greed that Independence has not changed.

In West Bengal, by 1983, the situation relating to the

invisible millions had to be considered, and it was perhaps naive to hope that any attempt by foreigners to do social work there was either practical, or possible. Foreigners are defined in Section 2(A) of the Foreigners Act 1946 as those 'who are not citizens of India', and the Act 'regulates and restricts the presence or continued presence of a foreigner in India'. As an Act, it is both separate and distinct from The Extradition Act of 1903, and it was under Section 14 of the Foreigners Act that the doctor was originally arrested in July 1981.

Persistent opposition and pressure by the Government of West Bengal, 'albeit embarrassed' as the editor of *The Statesman* Mr Sunanda Datta-Ray observed in 1982, is making charity work as difficult as it could be. It exerts pressure on relief schemes, organisations and individuals: all those, in fact, whose aim it is to help the poorest of the poor, the suffering, the starving, and others in need, who make up the invisible millions, that perhaps the Government would rather forget.

Giovanni Fonseca has written, 'The whole structure of society in India, with her population of 690 millions, may be visualised as a pyramid. Thirteen million are at the apex, followed by eighty million well-off. Below these are 297 million struggling to keep above the poverty line.'

Those whose welfare is both sound and assured, i.e. the better-off, are not greatly interested in the alteration of the class or caste system or in the redistribution of wealth, or improvements that will in any way jeopardise their own bastions of power, and their material satisfaction. To them missionaries may represent, in the long term, winds of change, and are thus a threat to the fabric of their society. Therefore they do not view them sympathetically.

In Calcutta alone, in the 'City of Dreadful Night' as Kipling called it, with its back-cloth of teeming millions, (thirteen million is the official estimate) Mother Teresa calculates one million of these as destitutes, or pavement dwellers. Slum dwellers total three million, but to be able to live in a slum you have to be able to pay for a room. You have to be able to earn the rent. The ten per cent official unemployment figure is probably too modest, if the working population in the city is fully assessed.

Many of the destitutes are refugees from Bihar, Orissa, and Bangladesh, where the genocide figures, according to Leo Kuper, in 1971 were an estimated three million. A further eight million sought refuge in West Bengal. All these people fall outside the Government's rehabilitation plans.

On July 26th, 1980, the *Tablet* in London reported that the work of charities in India was being restricted by the West Bengal Government, and noted the protest made by the eight Catholic bishops of West Bengal including Cardinal Lawrence Picarchy, Archbishop of Calcutta, and Chairman of the Indian Bishops' Conference. This protest took the form of a statement dated July 1st, 1980, later published in the Calcutta *Herald* on July 11th 1980. 'As Indian citizens,' the bishops wrote, 'while the Government of this country has the right to regulate the entry, residence and movements of foreigners, including foreign missionaries, we request the Government not to place more restrictions on foreign missionaries than are necessary.' The statement went on to point out their resentment at 'the growing tendency among certain sectors of the press and a few Government officials to blame the Christians and Christian missionaries for almost any unrest or trouble that occurs, especially in the Tribal Areas. Such an attitude very often aggravates an already sensitive situation and disturbs communal harmony which is essential for peace in India.'

Earlier, in another statement, an account of which was printed in the Indian Patna newspaper, *Amrita Bazar Pratika* dated June 22nd 1980, Cardinal Lawrence Picarchy wrote that statements by certain organisations that Christian missionaries were fermenting trouble in the North Eastern region of West Bengal were uncalled for.

The Chief Minister of West Bengal, Mr Jyoti Basu, sent his reply to the statement of the seven bishops in the form of a letter to the Cardinal. It was published on July 18th by the Calcutta *Herald*. In his answer the Chief Minister emphasised that the Government was not going to place more restrictions than were necessary. It added 'However, the State Government has to keep a watch on the activities of foreign-financed organisations in sensitive areas and take corrective action, whenever necessary, in consultation with the Government of India.'

The twelve agencies to be restricted were well known and included the non-denominational 'Care'; Caritas, the Catholic Relief Service of the Archdiocese of Calcutta; and CRS, an American organisation. These agencies were banned from starting new welfare programmes in Tribal Areas. Also affected by the prohibition were Oxfam, The Salvation Army, and Mother Teresa's Missionaries of Charity.

When reporters from Reuters and the BBC relayed the news that Mother Teresa's Mission was included in the list of banned organisations, it provoked a storm of protest resulting in an announcement by the Chief Minister that Mother Teresa's work was not subject to any restrictions whatever. Mother Teresa in fact had no schemes in the Tribal Areas; but she has Leprosy Homes at Midnapore and Asanol.

The ban was announced by the Minister for Tribal Welfare, Mr Sambu Mandi. Evidently the West Bengal Government link separatist movements in these areas with foreign charitable organisations. They also showed concern over the possibility of connections between elements in neighbouring Assam with foreign agencies.

The Government decree was due to take effect on July 31st, 1980, after which date it would itself be administering the foreign funds of these agencies. On December 5th, 1980, the Calcutta *Statesman* reported that the Government had also issued a circular to its officials telling them they must not have any ties with welfare organisations receiving funds from abroad.

The position regarding missionaries in the State of West Bengal is a delicate one. Basically the system accepts them on one hand, while it excludes them on the other. Missionaries of long standing are allowed to continue their work and maintain their schools, hospitals, dispensaries, etc. However, the latest move by the West Bengal Government restricting the growth of charitable organisations does not suggest improving relations. The policy is to let existing missionaries finish their term of office, or retire through old age, but not to allow others to take their place. In the disturbed states of North East India, Assam has only two Catholic missionaries, while the States of Mizoram, Arunchal Pradesh, Manipur, and Tripura have none. The case of the State of Arunchal Pradesh is of particular interest because permits to enter are also refused to priests and ministers. In Arunchal Pradesh, the Freedom of Religion Act decrees: 'No person shall convert, either directly or otherwise, any person from one religious faith to another religious faith'. In a report presented at the Catholic Bishops' Conference of India, Secretary General Bishop Joseph Thumma of Vivayawada stated that they were apprehensive about prohibitive legislation on freedom of religion, along the lines

131

taken in Arunchal Pradesh where harassment of Christians takes place. In Lethong, for example, village leaders were interrogated for hours by the District Commissioner because they had put up a church. In the village of Norfan they were accused of 'bringing a priest to their village'. The villagers were also offered a substantial bribe of 5000 rupees if they would state that their village had been visited by a priest without a permit. Countless other instances could be given of assault and harassment.

Other areas have been restricted by the West Bengal Government. In July 1980, the Chief Secretary of West Bengal told organisations in Jhargam to sever links with those areas. The Government proposed taking over schools, dispensaries, and training centres from the end of August. They were allowing no new programmes in Mindapore, Purulia, or Bankura districts.

The witch hunts in the North Eastern States made a nonsense of the concept of religious freedom enshrined in the Constitution of India, the founding fathers of which intended a secular and democratic republic.

The 'hidden hand', and foreign money, are the scapegoats of the Government when seeking a way out of a difficult situation. It is hard to gauge how much the Government's actions and the current situation result from the events of 1979 when Mr Tyagi's 'Freedom of Religion Bill' was on the Statute Book in the Lok Sabha, in New Delhi. The purpose of the proposed 'Freedom of Religion Bill' was to try to bring in legislation that would give the authorities a legal right to forbid missionary work in any given area.

That this manoeuvre, if it became law, could be used with great effect was clearly a fear in the minds of many in 1979, including four men of high position who in a series of articles defined their fears, and showed that the measure was both ill-conceived and ill-timed. The former Mayor Bombay went so far as to say that the proposed Bill, if passed, 'would add one more nail to the coffin of the Janata Party.'

The Constitution, which had given safeguards to the religious and educational institutions of minorities, would, if the Bill was made law, find those safeguards gone.

By 1983 feeling against missionaries was running high in Calcutta. The term missionary is used for anyone engaged in welfare work, be it of a denominational or non-denominatonal organisation, or secular, or purely humanitarian as in the case of Dr Preger. When I was interrogated by Security Control I was asked repeatedly whether I knew any missionaries.

Fear is at the heart of much of this repression. Many are afraid of the emergence of a Christian state. Certain conversions have taken place over the years among *Advasis,* the backward and scheduled classes and scheduled tribes. This fear is present in the prejudices of Hindu organisation like the RSS (Rashtriya Swayam Sevaka) and Hindu Mahasabla and the Ram Raj Parishad.

In February 1983 in Calcutta when the annual Book Fair was held one of the bookstalls had for distribution a thick typescript entitled *Missionaries As Enemy*, which held forth in great detail on the activities of the 'so-called Voluntary Organisations of West Bengal' including Oxfam and the Lutheran World Service.

The document was divided into various sections, under headings that coloured the opinions presented; there was the perennial 'Foreign Hand' and 'Aid as Imperialism' and it went on to list, in fifteen formidable sentences, a catalogue of indictments, all in one tone and similar to others in the text of the same genre. One of them reads 'Aid is fraud'. The source is quoted as *'Enemy*, by Felix Greene', (with no further details given.) It gave details of the fruits of surveillance of the missionaries by the Government and its detective department; the registration numbers of cars and motorcycles were given, with the whereabouts of odd copies of the Bible in polythene bags, which were sighted from time to time. In one section the document praised some relief work done during the severe floods, and then asked 'What for?' But the clue lay in the concluding paragraph which stated 'It is inevitable that those who provide a bowl of rice to the hungry and needy will certainly take a chance of the situation to exploit them when the time comes.'

Clearly the work of all voluntary organisations is suspect in the eyes of the Government, so that it is actively taking steps to terminate it where possible. In doing so they make great difficulties for themselves, adding financial burdens if the work is to be maintained, and creating unrest if hitherto-aided people are deprived.

It is possible, however, that there is some truth in the allegations of the West Bengal Government. The overall picture is an extremely complicated one, involving current politics and the fears that must always be present to the Government of a sub-continent with such a border. It is a border, albeit of unsurpassed beauty containing the most superb mountain range in the world, the Himalayas, that is shared with Afghanistan in the West, and the massive Chinese border. This, like the palm of an outstretched hand, caresses the frozen slopes of the North and the North-Eastern approaches to India, touching the North-Western States of Jammu and Kashmir, Nepal and Assam.

Some light on the tangled web of bureaucracy in West Bengal has been shed by Sunanda Datta-Ray of the *Statesman*. In a long article entitled 'Government by Suspicion', which was published in India in September 1981, and in London in the *Observer*, he argues that the Government in West Bengal is ridden by an irrational fear of foreigners. He shows how this deteriorating situation leads the government in Calcutta into deeper waters, and also involves the Central Government in New Delhi. He cites three examples in which one British and two American nationals with unblemished records have been asked to leave India.

This does not mean that India's customary courtesy in dealing with foreigners is in any way relaxed; authorities and civil servants still behave in a sympathetic manner, but this does not prevent Government policies being implemented with speed.

In November, 1981, I had to present myself to Security Control for questioning. They questioned me for hours, but were polite. When the first part was over I was referred to the higher levels of Security Control, appropriately higher up in the building, and I climbed the curving dusty staircase to the District Commissioner's room. He was a Sikh, and good looking in his maroon turban. He sat behind a large semi-circular desk on a slight dais and I sat in front. He was painstakingly correct and polite, nevertheless he enquired into every aspect of every detail of my life during the past months in Calcutta, with a very direct line of questioning relating to the work with destitutes. Perhaps as an unconscious psychological defence I countered his probing with a rather long soliloquy on the position of the destitute in Indian society.

In 1982 Security Control became persistent in their surveillance. The Co-Workers of Mother Teresa's were in the limelight. One of them, Dr Imelda Buigan, was hounded out of

134

the voluntary medical teaching course that she was giving to the sisters of the Missionaries of Charity, by being followed everywhere, which was part of the usual pattern of harassment. Another was put under house arrest, and left, by agreement. An English television production manager had to leave after working at Kalighat, Mother Teresa's Home for the Dying. So did an American teacher, and a German midwife, and then, later in the year, Michael Morony, the son of a British general.

When I returned from my second visit to England I was followed continually by as many as four 'shadows' at a time. In January 1983 surveillance reached a peak. It was the week when I was left an official note instructing me to report to Security Control, and to consider the matter as urgent. When I went there, they took a statement from me, which took about two and a half hours. The doctor came with me and also insisted that a solicitor should attend. This solicitor was known to the authorities apart from the fact that he was acting on the doctor's behalf and had appeared in court for him already. We were ushered in, guided along the passage past the file-lined walls that I remembered well from 1981. Jack remained out in the hall, sitting on one of the ex-car seats provided as chairs. As the SC officer knew the lawyer, he was permitted to enter the office but he would not, they said, be allowed to speak because the proceedings were 'secret'.

I sat there in a room full of desks, behind which no work appeared to be going on; there was a lot of chatting, and interest in the direction of my interrogator. He fired a lot of questions at me, the first being more in the nature of a statement: "The doctor is a missionary."

To this I answered: "An alleged missionary."

"Why the legal language?" he asked.

"Because," I answered, "he is not a missionary — and because it's not proven."

He went on to ask about my relationship with Jack, where I lived, and why I was here. Then he returned to my file, and brought up the question of the proposed Programme for the Relief of Pavement Dwellers. I had done a lot of work for this in 1981, and had almost got a committee together. Unfortunately when I was nearly ready to get it registered in India, I had been warned by Security Control that I probably would not be allowed to remain in India anyway. This was confirmed by a member of the Legislative Assembly, who had helped us over several problems of getting destitutes admitted to hospital, including Kala. He warned me that my name was on a list of those to be ordered to leave. He would not therefore agree to serve on my committee, and I had no option but to drop the project. The interrogating officer said he would write in the statement that I had given up the idea after talking to Mr Singh in 1981. I told him, no, the truth was that I could not proceed because I was going to be ordered to leave India. He agreed to record what I said, but his alternative, he said, would have helped me.

The questions had gone on and on. My passport, which I had handed over, was studied at great length. At one point someone came in and mentioned that the doctor was waiting in the hall. At this news a great fuss was made about their friend the doctor, who was duly fetched in. They brought a chair and placed it next to mine. Then they repeated to him a question to which I had not known the answer. Attention was diverted to the doctor, and, the questions at last apparently over, I held out my hand for the return of my passport. My interrogator thought I was going to shake hands. ''My passport,'' I explained, and presently it was returned to me.

CHAPTER XI

IN CONCLUSION

The greatest perserverance is perserverance without reward

Prior of Taizé

CHAPTER XI

In Conclusion

THE future of the pavement people, if they were deprived by the imprisonment or deportation of their doctor by the Government of West Bengal, would be grave. Such an action would underline the hopelessness of their position and the day he was no longer with them would bring with it a fresh onslaught from their ills, be they long term diseases or the misery of a skin infection to be borne with no chance of relief. Nor, unless steps were taken by the West Bengal Government, would it bring any improvement in their material lot.

To exchange a few square feet of filthy cracked pavement in Calcutta for open land to work and ground to till, a hut in which to live, or medical care, are things which one must constantly remember as realisable hopes. Christopher Columbus knew, was convinced, that the world was round — so he discovered America. One knows that these alternatives are not only possibilities, but the answer to all the people's prayers, which day by day they keep in the depths of their hearts. Is it any wonder then, that they love the man who shares these hopes for them, and who, as long as it is humanly possible to work for these objectives, will not fail them?

It is interesting to pose the hypothetical question that forms in many people's minds when considering the position of one single individual standing his ground in the face of continuing government pressure, and ask: how much easier would it be for Dr Preger to leave, and go to another corner of the world? There is no shortage of the poor, the sick and the dying; nor of refugees: men, women and children, to be cared for; nor places where the presence of a qualified and experienced doctor would be welcome.

When Jack Preger walks among the people he looks after does he question the reasons for being there? Does he ask himself 'Have I made a mistake by coming here?' Does he reflect that if he looks after these people they represent only a few thousand among millions? And that when one dies there is always another to take his place? No, he does not ask these questions, for he believes if one patient dies and there is another to take his place, that is all the more reason why he must be there. If it appears hopeless, then we have made it so, including those of us in the developed world. All these convictions are based on assessments of true values, as he sees them. That he remains working on the streets can only be seen as fearlessness born out of a deep-rooted inner strength, which is why Jack Preger continues on his hard course.

Without his help what would be the chances for these people? Would the West Bengal Government undertake to give the destitute of that area free medical attention and hospital beds? Would it supply invalid carriages for cripples and polio victims? Would the Government of Bangladesh allow its citizens now living in the flyover vicinity to return to their own country? At one time the Indian High Commission acknowledged the existence of the Bangladeshi families in the Strand Road area of Calcutta by suggesting that the matter be taken up with the Bangladesh Government. Three letters dated March 3rd 1983, relating to this and other matters, had been sent; two, directly for the attention of General H. M. Ershad in Dhaka, and finally one dated March 7th, 1984, to the Bangladesh Government through its High Commissioner in London, at the High Commission for the Bangladesh People's Republic. But the High Commission for the People's Republic of Bangladesh in London denies having a record of any Bangladeshi citizens stranded in Calcutta. Back in 1978, before any of this correspondence, the doctor had tried to get permission from the Government of India to set up a programme in Calcutta for destitutes.

The situation of the flyover people is now more desperate because of the construction of enormous railings at the flyover and Strand Road area barring them from many of the places where they used to live. It is increasingly urgent to get negotiations opened with the Bangladesh Government and the

Indian Government in the hope of getting them to repatriate the Bangladeshi families.

On January 21st, 1984, the Calcutta *Telegraph* carried a report that 400,000 Muslim Biharis in Bangladesh would be repatriated to Pakistan over the next three years, even though these Biharis had never been in Pakistan before. If that is possible in Pakistan perhaps Bangladesh will accept her own destitutes, provided we can raise funds to pay for their resettlement. The numbers of the flyover people directly involved are not enormous; approximately a hundred families. By 1988 there were some grounds for hope about this.

Meanwhile, the authorities continue, from time to time, to raid the flyover people and try to move them out. The *Telegraph* on February 3rd, 1984, reported that a seven year old girl had been killed by a tram on route 12a on the Calcutta side of Howrah Bridge approach. Traffic was disrupted for half an hour, the police said, because a commotion had followed the accident.

What was not reported was that on the same day some Calcutta Corporation employees were sent under the Strand Road flyover, where the girl had died, to burn the possessions of the squatters there, most of them the illegal immigrants from Bangladesh who so badly needed to be repatriated. These were people who, if resettled, could be given a communal farming programme — if the doctor were allowed to recover and use the land he purchased in Bangladesh but that has been confiscated by the Bangladesh Government in 1979 without compensation. Only continuing perseverance on his part and the part of others like him can change the situation for these people or open the eyes of others to the facts.

St Augustine said 'act as though everything depends on you, pray as if everything depends on God'. There can be no separation in our understanding of this. There is no other way that the strength required can be found, other than at its root in God and the Holy Spirit, however hidden from day and from others it may be. At the ground of all change, that is the renewing force.

Jack Preger has stated to the authorities, categorically, that he is prepared to pursue indefinitely the moral right that he considers he has, to work with the Calcutta destitutes; this is coupled with the belief that if he is prevented from working with them he will not accept this prohibition. If deported he would try to return to India, and re-enter legally as a Commonwealth citizen. Then he would apply for permission (as he did in 1979) to the West Bengal Government to allow him to work with the pavement dwellers and go to Security Control to register, also as he did in 1979. If, however, he is again refused entry to India, and is again deported, he has promised to return and seek to re-enter illegally — without passing through any immigration post. Then, the whole process would start again. He would go to a lawyer at once and afterwards to Security Control, possibly to face re-arrest and imprisonment. If allowed out on bail and if the next trial showed any prospect of being a lengthy one, he would again start work. He thinks that this action would be a constructive path in demonstrating the moral right which he believes he has to work with the Calcutta destitutes. Also, he would be drawing attention to the necessity of providing medical care for these people. If, and this should be clearly understood, the destitute were properly cared for, then he would be happy to work elsewhere, wherever he might be most needed. His hope, always, is to see the fulfilment of his long term aim, the repatriation of the Bangladeshi families and a medical programme serving both West Bengal and Bangladesh.

FOR his friends, and for the destitute, imprisonment for Jack Preger has to be regarded as an evil. A long prison sentence would undoubtedly bring about a serious deterioration in his physical health for after less than two weeks' imprisonment in Alipore Special Jail in 1981, where the food was appalling in quality, he came out weakened, and very soon fell ill, with the distress of a badly broken tooth and with amoebic dysentery. He suffered for four and a half months. What a longer term in prison would hold in store, if the pattern of 1981 were to be repeated, cannot be dismissed lightly, for he would be living without anti-malaria medication, with poor food and inadequate sanitation, sleeping, if it were possible, shoulder to shoulder on a cell floor with forty other men.

For the doctor, to accept these possibilities of harrassment and imprisonment, as an alternative to a normal peaceful life spent pursuing his professional medical work in another corner of the globe, illustrates the degree of conviction with which he holds his profound views about the care and well-being of the living destitute whom he serves.

JUNG talks about our collective unconscious. In this, he suggests, we hold the intuitions of the past that make up our present selves, and in which are contained the sources of our present actions, whether we are aware of these things or not. So the past must hold a key to help us to understand his deep commitment to these people. Certainly his faith is clearly apparent, but his association with the poor and sick seems to have, beyond compassion even, some other sense. As a child Jack Preger was told his family was suffering in Germany, some in prison camps, and when he first entered the Bihari Refugee Camps in 1972 he felt they were familiar to him, as if he recognised them from the past he had never seen.

His mother appears in the doctor's conversations as a person who was courageous under the ordeal of questioning by the Nazis just before the onset of World War Two. I feel that there is a good deal of her influence in his life, quite apart from the Jewish background. Born in what was East Poland (now Russia) where her grandfather had a small farm, she lived there until she was three years old when she went to live in Bavaria. Later she came to England. Some of her family managed to leave Germany in time to flee to England, some were persecuted, hiding on separate farms, each thinking the others dead. Some died in concentration camps. She went back to Bavaria just before the war to get her parents out and while she was there all the Jews in her home town of Fürth were rounded up and made to witness the burning of their synagogue. She was released only because she held a British passport. So, it is not surprising that he identified closely with the persecuted Bihari Muslim refugees who poured into the camps in Bangladesh after the 1971 war. Many of them are still there, or with the destitute in a dreadful vagrants home in Bangladesh.

POVERTY has no frontiers. In a pre-Easter 1984 interview on BBC Television in England, Bishop David Sheppard of Liverpool discussed social matters in the Dimbleby Lecture of that name. Bishop Sheppard's message was that there is a poverty which imprisons the spirit, and he went on to enlarge on this in relation to current industrial unrest in Britain. This poverty which imprisons the spirit is the imprisonment that Christ came to change, that Isaiah spoke of, and that St Luke quotes: 'He has sent me to proclaim release to the captives, to set at liberty those who are oppressed'. Those who are oppressed are so often God's people; the imprisoned, the refugees, who look out at the world from behind the wire fences of their camps. Consider those tortured in the cellars of Central America today, and in the gulags of Russia; in the fastnesses of Gestapo HQs in World War II yesterday, and in the ghettos of Poland, where the stark truth and simplicity of Vishnaic's black and white photographs have captured forever the suffering of Jewish children and families;* and the silent, numbing agony of both old and young starving in stricken areas throughout the world.

In the minds of those oppressed by life, there is another form of imprisonment. There is a loneliness in the heart of a child playing ball in the enclosed playground of a modern orphanage, an emptiness in the souls of the drug addicts and of the shutouts of western society, as Mother Teresa calls them, who exist in the skyscraper landscape of downtown Chicago.

Christ and Isaiah would recognise the need for all these people to be set free.

Like a shadow over every attempt to improve the lot of the socially deprived in India hangs the question of 'untouchability'. As Gandhi said, 'untouchability is a terrible reality', and it has a bearing on the whole issue of poverty and the position of the destitute in Indian society. It lies at the root of all social problems there. I put it to Jack Preger that until this is in some way overcome the difficulties he faces are unlikely to be resolved. Basically, the Government of West Bengal is acutely embarrassed by the whole issue of poverty. To this he answered: "There is one way of carrying on Gandhi's teaching, an important way. In my opinion Gandhi did not succeed, and I am sure I will not either, in trying to apply his concepts, but I am not attached to 'success'. Doing the obvious thing in this appalling situation is enough; and God gives us, in our weakness, victories every day, just to keep us going. We should not need these to be encouraged, but they are there."

With the doctor, I believe that the leper waiting on the pavement outside the Y in Calcutta is there for me. I am not there for him.

The word solidarity is one that is being coined by trade unions and groups of people all across the globe. The dictionary definition is 'holding together, mutual dependence'. There is

*Photographs contained in the book *A Vanished World* by Roman Vishnaic.

just such a solidarity beginning to emerge clearly in the work of churches of all denominations, among social workers and large humanitarian organisations like Oxfam, Help the Aged, the Cheshire Homes, and many others. These have often started, as in the case of the Cheshire Homes, with an event that has left a scar both on the world and on a particular individual. Group Captain Leonard Cheshire is one such man, who after his involvement with the dropping of the atomic bomb on the two Japanese cities of Hiroshima and Nagasaki, found himself profoundly and understandably influenced in his subsequent life and thought. As a result, he has produced a counter to the horror of that annihilation, a life devoted to the help of thousands of invalid people.

This is the other side of the coin of modern repression, victimisation and neglect; the currency of care that has its beginnings in the individuals and religious houses and orders from earlier Christian centuries, and that has come down to us through the continuation of the motive force of these in the great supportive and reforming figures of people such as Wilberforce, Nightingale and Shaftesbury. It has been backed in the field of literature by Dickens' portrayal of nineteenth century life, and by artists and illustrators such as Doré and Cruikshank and, before them, Rowlandson and Hogarth. It has been reinforced by moves for change in government policy, in industry, and other institutions. All this has now, almost at the end of the twentieth century, come to a flowering in the scene of world poverty, social welfare, and human rights.

There is certainly a new awareness of the poverty of the Third World among the general public. No doubt this is related to some extent to communications, and reforming societies, and always, as from the beginning, there is the work of outstanding individuals like the Nobel Prize winners Albert Schweitzer and Mother Teresa of Calcutta. Men like Raoul Wallenberg have broken new ground in determining ideals that can never be overestimated. Repeatedly the emphasis is on saving human life, establishing and maintaining the dignity of the refugee, the destitute, the prisoner either in the physical sense, or the mental.

WHAT has happened in the mind of Jack Preger since those first encounters that are described in the Prologue and which made such an impression on him?

145

Since those earlier days his position has been a gradual movement towards the liberation movement in the Church. "The Spirit may well have pushed me into the Church," Dr Preger says, "but with some intensity I find myself heading away from the ritualism of church services, etc., and towards worshipping Christ in the poor."

Jack Preger could be said to have been influenced firstly by what he calls the charismatic events in his life, which have brought him to where he stands to-day. He is, however, now clearly and more strongly identifying with the oppressed, and has sympathy with people such as the Jesuits, whose attitude in relation to Central American politics has been criticised by the Pope. But he continues to hold, and adhere closely to, the spirit of St Paul, with his belief in the power of the Holy Spirit and primarily in God.

He is a complex man, very much of his century, on whom the present influence of the Church in Central America has some bearing and who follows to some extent the new Church that springs from the people and that is personified in the poor. However, India is by no means parallel to Christian and Catholic Central America, because in India predominantly the population is Hindu and Muslim, with Christians and Catholics as a very small minority.

Here again, in the doctor's mind, there has been an opening-out since those early days of the first charismatic experiences; there is a growing awareness of and openness to other religions.

Christ was explicit about the force of the spirit in the hands of his disciples. Maybe in our hands too. After all the years passed in contact with Muslims, Buddhists and Hindus, Jack Preger thinks, like Evans-Wentz, Miro and Jung, increasingly, that Christ came for all men because He was, is and shall be a conduit for the Spirit, that the Spirit was before the beginning and will be forever, and that we are a part of it. So accordingly, he also believes in re-incarnation. Jack Preger finds a basis for working in Calcutta only in an amalgam of Christianity, Hinduism, Buddhism, and Islam. On the surface they have a great number of contradictions and absurdities. But in their depths they possess not only great beauty, but also the truth.

JACK PREGER has one allegiance that has its place in the continuing story; that of a devotion to St Antony of Padua. He

146

feels that St Antony is particularly concerned with the poor in Calcutta, in response to the prayers of the Anglo-Indians there to him. Dr Preger's own prayers to St Antony, just prior to his arrest by the West Bengal Government in July 1981, were 'resoundingly answered'. This was after he had stopped to pray that day at the St Joseph's Chapel in Market Street, a narrow side street just a few minutes from the Newmarket; both those who attend Mass at the chapel and those who visit it, usually have a great devotion to the saint. In the little pamphlet which one can buy in the church, it describes St Antony's qualities as resembling those of St Joseph, which provide for our spiritual and temporal wants. It also explains the practice of St Antony's Bread, when answered prayers are acknowledged by gifts of bread, to be given out to the poor in due course.

So often in that chapel the candles burning there, placed in front of the life-sized figure of St Antony in his niche between simple marble columns and architrave, are thinner than the thinnest little finger. Brilliant stars of light, these candles burn, symbolic of prayers for the poor, their children, the sick, the dead and the living; for the trivial and for the important, all are valid.

That the doctor was allowed to remain in Calcutta and was not deported from West Bengal, was his answered prayer. But that prayer is constantly renewed, constantly requiring answer; for it, candles still burn before the statue, not only in Calcutta but in other countries also, before other statues of that saint who bears the Christ child in his arms. They burn not only for personal temporal wants but for those of others, that for the sake of the poor in Calcutta their doctor, Jack Preger, may be allowed to continue to work in their city.

Mother and Child

Bibliography

THE NEW ENGLISH BIBLE. Cambridge University Press.
  Oxford University Press.
Andrew Boyle. *NO PASSING GLORY*. Collins. 1983 (Paperback edition)
Dom Heldar Camara. *SPIRAL OF VIOLENCE*
  Dimension Books. New Jersey, 1971
Sukharanjan Dasgupta. *MIDNIGHT MASSACRE IN DACCA*
  Vikas Publishing House, India
THE DHAMMAPADA. Introduction and translation from the Pali by Juan
  Mascaro. Penguin Classics
John S. Dunne. *THE REASONS OF THE HEART*. SCM Press. 1978
THE LIFE OF MAHATMA GANDHI. Louis Fisher. 1982. Granada
EPIGRAMS FROM GANDHIJI. Compiled by S. R. Tikehar. Published by
  Government of India Press
Dudley Gardiner. *ANGEL WITH A BUSHY BEARD*. St. Andrew's Press.
  1980
Hilda C. Graef. *THE SCHOLAR AND THE CROSS*. Longman Green & Co.
  1955
Günter Grass. *THE FLOUNDER*. Radhakrisha Prakashan. 1979
Dom Bede Griffiths. *THE MARRIAGE OF EAST AND WEST*
  1982. Collins. London
Brian Griffiths. *IS REVOLUTION CHANGE*. Inter-Varsity Press. 1972
Herman Hesse. *DAMAIN*. Panther Books. First published in G.B. 1960 by
  Peter Owen and Vision Press
I CHING, OR BOOK OF CHANGES. Foreword G. C. Jung.
  Princetown Univeristy Press. 1978
William Johnston. *SILENT MUSIC*. Collins. Fount Paperback. 1974
JUNG AND THE STORY OF OUR TIME. Laurens van der Post
  The Hogarth Press. 1976
Rudyard Kipling. *CITY OF DREADFUL NIGHT*
Larry Collins Dominique Lapierre. *FREEDOM AT MIDNIGHT*
  Bell Books. Vikas P.H. India 1976
Mary Ellen Mark. *FALKLAND ROAD*. Thames & Hudson. 1981
Malcolm Muggeridge. *SOMETHING BEAUTIFUL FOR GOD*
  Collins. London. 1971
NAGEL'S ENCYCLOPAEDIA GUIDE TO INDIA AND NEPAL
Raimundo Panikkar. *THE VEDIC EXPERIENCE*. D.T.L. 1977
PONTIFF. Gordon Thomas & Max Morgan Witts. Granada 1983
Apostolic Exhortation of Pope John Paul II. *REDEMPTIONIS DONUM*.
  C.T.S. 1984
Salman Rushdie. *MIDNIGHT'S CHILDREN*. Avon Books. U.S.A. April
  1982
Roger Schutz, Prior of Taizé. *VIOLENT FOR PEACE*. (Translation by
  C.J. Moore). Darton, Longman and Todd. 1970
R.B. Seth. *LAW OF THE FOREIGNERS AND CITIZENSHIP*
  Illard Edition. Law Publishers. Allahabad. 1981
Hugh Clarke. *EDITH STEIN*. C.T.S. 1984
Simone Weil. *WAITING ON GOD*. Routledge, Kegan & Paul. 1951
Abbot William of St Thierry. *THE GOLDEN EPISTLE*
  Sheed & Ward. 1930 and 1980

Papers by Dr Jack Preger
and Newspaper, Periodical, Radio and
TV References

'The Sheep and Goats'. *The Tablet.* 1979.
'Calcutta's Destitute'. *The Tablet.* 23rd January 1982.
'Bengal Vagrants'. August 1983.
'Alipore Special Jail. In Memoriam'. August 24th, 1983.

The following have carried articles or features on Doctor Preger's work, written by himself, or by journalists.

ENGLAND
The Daily Telegraph. London
New Internationalist. London
The Observer. London
Private Eye. London
The Tablet. London
The Times. London
Interview with Mark Tully, BBC. Filmed in India in 1982
Channel Four TV documentary: *34 Middleton Row; The Jack Preger Story*

U.S.A.
The People

DENMARK
Ugebladet Hjemmet. Copenhagen

SWITZERLAND
24 Heures

BANGLADESH
Bangladesh Times
The Hindustan Times
New Nation

INDIA
All India Reporter. 1982. (Law Report re Adoptions)
All India Reporter. 1883. Supreme Court
Amrita Bazar Patrika
The Business Standard
Frontier
The Herald. Calcutta
Holiday
Link Magazine
The Statesman. Calcutta
Sunday
The Sunday Observer. Bombay
The Telegraph. Calcutta